Rhetoric and Technical Communication in HOPE VI

Rhetoric and Technical Communication in HOPE VI

An Analysis of Race and Participatory Capture in U.S. Housing

Christopher J. Morris

LEXINGTON BOOKS
Lanham • Boulder • New York • London

Published by Lexington Books
An imprint of The Rowman & Littlefield Publishing Group, Inc.
4501 Forbes Boulevard, Suite 200, Lanham, Maryland 20706
www.rowman.com

86-90 Paul Street, London EC2A 4NE, United Kingdom

British Library Cataloguing in Publication Information Available

Library of Congress Cataloging-in-Publication Data

Names: Morris, Christopher Jerone, author.
Title: Rhetoric and technical communication in HOPE VI : an analysis of race and participatory capture in U.S. housing / Christopher Morris.
Description: Lanham : Lexington Books, [2025] | Includes bibliographical references and index. | Summary: "This book provides a rhetorical analysis of HOPE VI, a federal mixed-income, public housing program. The author addresses the phenomenon of participatory capture that worsened inequality, prompting a reconsideration, rhetorical and otherwise, of what it means to participate in America's cities"— Provided by publisher.
Identifiers: LCCN 2024032958 (print) | LCCN 2024032959 (ebook) | ISBN 9781666946857 (cloth ; alk. paper) | ISBN 9781666946864 (epub)
Subjects: LCSH: Public housing—United States. | Low-income housing—United States. | Discrimination—United States. | Urban renewal—United States. | Rhetoric—Political aspects—United States. | United States. Department of Housing and Urban Development.
Classification: LCC HD7288.78.U5 M66 2025 (print) | LCC HD7288.78.U5 (ebook) | DDC 363.5/850973—dc23/eng/20240903
LC record available at https://lccn.loc.gov/2024032958
LC ebook record available at https://lccn.loc.gov/2024032959

∞™ The paper used in this publication meets the minimum requirements of American National Standard for Information Sciences—Permanence of Paper for Printed Library Materials, ANSI/NISO Z39.48-1992.

Contents

List of Tables

Preface

I didn't know what it meant to be an uncanny guest until I returned to my childhood home—one of them anyway. Standing on the side of the road, taking in the tiny brick, two-bedroom pre-war on the edge of Pittsburgh's Penn Hills, I was both there and not.

This feeling of uncanniness can be described as "when the home is invaded by one's own doppelgänger, there is an indication that the home invasion comes from within, that the home is not as comforting as believed in the first place" (Cameron 2020). Home for me was complicated. As a child, I lived with my single mother and older brother in a row house in Homewood—what was then (and still is) a predominantly low-income Black neighborhood in Pittsburgh, where crime, drugs, and urban blight were steady conditions. At the same time, almost my entire family lived in Homewood, with my grandmother having migrated to Pittsburgh from Alabama in the earlier half of the twentieth century.

With her, she brought the culture and perseverance that sustained generations before and after. The Homewood I grew up in was rough (still is), yet alongside the negative were everyday love, warmth, support, and activity—first days of school, summer camps, graduations, family reunions, holiday parties, church services and Sunday dinners, birthday parties, and little league football games—that nurtured families and neighbors.

My own mother's journey was one that went up-and-down in tandem with the duality of urban America. She spent her childhood in the Homewood-Brushton projects before moving to the row houses on Susquehanna Street with her two young sons. The row houses and their surrounding area were targeted for redevelopment some years later, and my mother received public assistance to move into a house in the Pittsburgh suburb of Penn Hills.

Sometime thereafter, she became a mother a third time. As all of these changes took place in her home life, she remained unmarried with uneven job prospects.

As we moved, so did everyone else in my family. They were displaced not just by the redevelopment and relocation efforts of the city but also by the growing untenability of living in an area that continually offered less and less in the way of security and peace. Amid this movement, family bonds fractured, elders passed, and the glue—geographic or otherwise—that held us together began to dissolve. Initially, my mother threw a big party to celebrate her move to Penn Hills. For her, the new home represented opportunities for stability and happiness. Family and friends, with food and housewarming gifts, met the 960-square-foot single family with pride and promise—a promise that ultimately never materialized.

While Homewood sustained us in various ways, the neighborhood also undermined us in others. My mother struggled with this tension. Alongside family and friends came crime and tumultuous relationships with men, both of which haunted her as she attempted to slip the millstones of the past. Within a couple of years of the move, both she and my older brother would end up spending time in jail. I moved in with my father, who faced his own challenges with finding a stable living situation, in a city with limited hopeful spaces for low-income, Black residents.

In December 2023, with some apprehension, I revisited my mother's Penn Hills home. My mother had died years ago from cancer at the age of fifty, and, for me, to confront her home again was to confront anew the reality of her life and memory amid my sense of loss. The house was smaller than I remembered, and against the backdrop of that day's gray clouds, something about the diminished brick seemed cruel. My memories could not transform the house into my mother's dreams for it. In the front window, the current occupant had put up a sign: "Protect Black Mothers."

Standing in front of the house, part of me wanted to knock on the door and meet the mother inside. I didn't dare, for fear that the woman in the house would be my mother, perfectly preserved as I remember her when she lived there—in one instance, beaming with joy as she cradled my newborn sister, and in another, crying at the bottom of the steps, saying, "Ever since I got this house, everything has gone wrong." My mother eventually found some stability, though she continued to live as a single mother from one low-income area in Pittsburgh to another on Section 8. I'd like to believe, before the end of her life, that she found some happiness in her steadfast love for family wherever hers dwelled.

This book is neither an autobiography nor a sociocultural study of urban decay and renewal. Both of those genres have spawned a rightful assortment of classics in American literature and academic research. Instead, this book is an attempt to wrestle with the inherent contradictions of American urban housing—indeed, its uncanniness—particularly for low-income Black residents whose places in U.S. cities seem both entrenched and wayward. For me, this uncanniness manifests perhaps most peculiarly in the concept of participation and especially the rhetoric that celebrates Black and low-income participation in urban redevelopment. As a writer, I'm interested in how the institutional forces that influenced so much of my family's contemporary history also told the stories of neighborhoods, cities, and of America itself. I, for one, know how some of those stories end and yet begin again in a state of participatory capture.

Acknowledgments

This book began as my dissertation project completed at The Ohio State University in 2021. I thank my dissertation committee for their invaluable support, guidance, and insight: Jonathan Buehl, Christa Teston, Wendy Hesford, and Shannon Winnubst.

Various parts of this book, including chapters 1 and 2, respectively, draw from my articles: "Participation, Diversity, and Legitimation in U.S. Housing: A Rhetorical Analysis of Two HOPE VI Reports" published in *Technical Communication* (2024); and "Race, Rhetoric, and Participatory Capture in U.S. Housing: Deficit and Governance Models in HOPE VI" published in *Organization* (2024). I thank the editors of those journals for helping me to clarify and strengthen my arguments.

For providing me with an indelible sense of home, I thank the neighborhood of Homewood as well as my family, including my greatest teachers: Lavetta Morris, Kathryn Carroll, and Jerone Morris.

Finally, I extend my warmest and sincerest thanks to Joshua Leavitt for his generous eyes on many drafts. Six words can never be enough.

Chapter 1

HOPE VI, Participatory Capture, and Technical Communication

As of 2024, the U.S. housing market could hardly be characterized by words like "hope" and "participation." Housing affordability, let alone homeownership, appears out of reach for millions. For a variety of reasons—ranging from zoning restrictions to income inequality—housing costs have significantly outpaced incomes (Saiz 2023). As a result of these economic dynamics, according to congressional testimony provided by the Center on Budget and Policy Priorities (2024), "more than half of cost-burdened renter households—12.1 million—pay more than 50 percent of their income on rent . . . an all-time high" and "On a single night in January 2023, 653,000 people were experiencing homelessness in the United States, a 12 percent increase from a year earlier and the highest number ever recorded." For Black residents, renters, and would-be homeowners, the lack of affordability remains especially acute.

Economic inequality as well as racial discrimination in both public and private housing policies have led to conditions wherein Black renters and homebuyers experience the nation's highest rates of evictions and homelessness. The Joint Center for Housing Studies reported that from 2021 to 2022, the number of Black renters who could afford median-priced housing fell 52 percent and that "In April 2021, 14.2 percent of all Black renter households could afford a home and by April 2022 just 6.9 percent of all Black renter households could afford the median-priced home" (Hanifa 2022). Housing affordability (or lack thereof), meanwhile, has significant impacts on public health, education, labor markets, and civic engagement. Ironically, this concerning state of affairs, in which the distinction between the haves and have-nots is so stark, is the public policy product of the HOPE VI era—a thirty-year period that, from approximately 1990–2020, saw the deliberate dismantling of public and affordable housing in favor of privatization and mortgage securitization. Perhaps even more ironic, as policymakers and stakeholders went about this dismantling, they mandated that the most vulnerable of those affected by these policies participate in their implementation. This book explores how elites—mainly at the level of the U.S. federal government—used the rhetoric of "participation" in public and technical writing to re-entrench inequality and to divest public housing residents of power, all while claiming to do the opposite.

HOPE VI (Housing Opportunities for People Everywhere) was a U.S. federal program that, from approximately 1992 to 2012, funded public housing demolition in favor of housing vouchers and privatized mixed-income developments that purported to emphasize citizen participation. More recently, similar federal programs have been implemented: Choice Neighborhoods (2010–present) and Opportunity Zones (2017–present). In response to concentrations of crime and poverty that affected public housing complexes and low-income communities by the late 1980s, the U.S. Department of Housing and Urban Development (HUD) committed to tearing down "the projects" and replacing them with more standalone, single-family homes. The initial stated goal of the program was to reduce the concentration of poverty and crime in public housing units. HUD also sought to deconcentrate poverty by giving vouchers to low-income residents to rent better-quality housing units in higher-income neighborhoods.

HOPE VI decreased publicly funded housing and instead supported urban redevelopment as well as low-income homeownership by expanding mortgage and credit markets—markets that policymakers continually deregulated and subsidized throughout the 1990s and early 2000s. In this way, HOPE VI and the subprime mortgage crisis were concurrent, interrelated developments. Hyra (2012) explains that during that time, "Credit for home purchase, once denied to black inner city areas, flowed into these communities at unprecedented rates and helped stimulate the inner city gentrification pattern" and that "Subprime originations, which disproportionately went to African-Americans, increased from $35 billion in 1994 to $625 billion in 2005" (508). Meanwhile, the subprime and often predatory loans were securitized and resold, accelerating the 2007–2008 financial crisis, as "Mortgage companies and commercial banks originating prime and subprime loans in inner city areas sold them to financial institutions that repackaged these pooled loans into mortgage-backed securities" (Hyra 2012, 508). The increase in homelessness and displacement brought about by HOPE VI was ultimately mirrored by the foreclosures and loss of wealth that disproportionately affected Black and low-income homeowners in the wake of the financial crisis.

In *Race for Profit*, Taylor (2019) traces this predatory, inclusionary/exclusionary dynamic back to the 1970s when federal housing laws were reformed to officially disallow racial discrimination in home lending. Around this same time, political will to enforce racial residential integration and publicly funded housing was low. Taylor argues that non-discriminatory lending laws "generated unprecedented real estate sales in Black urban communities across the country. But the transition from the exclusionary policies of HUD and the [Federal Housing Administration] to inclusion into the world of urban real estate sales was fraught with problems" (Taylor 2019, 3). Primarily, legal reforms did not overcome racially motivated profit incentives, since "The FHA's guaranteed mortgage, the subsidized interest rates, and the captured segregated housing market incentivized market actors to speculate that the poverty and desperation of Black urban residents, especially Black women, would drive them toward the low-income homeownership market" (Taylor 2019, 18). Ultimately, the persistence of racial segregation further contributed to the crime, neglect, and deterioration that characterized U.S. public housing through to the 1990s and that which provided the rhetorical and political exigencies to enact the HOPE VI era, the "new" urban renewal.

HUD's efforts resulted in thousands of affected low-income residents living in homelessness and a reconcentration of poverty in other areas. When HUD demolished public housing units and redeveloped communities with new houses, new retail, and social amenities, the Department reserved fewer new units for low-income residents than had existed prior to redevelopment. In stipulating its own institutional preferences for resident desirability, through appeals to diversity, HUD made admittance to the new developments contingent upon work requirements, drug tests, and criminal records. Lower-income residents who remained post development were eventually priced out of neighborhoods that experienced rising rents and expenses. At the same time, displaced residents who received vouchers to move to higher-income areas suffered a similar pricing-out effect and struggled also to adjust to demographically different neighborhoods. Meanwhile, HUD justified this approach by citing lower crime rates and rising incomes in the redeveloped areas. Those statistical successes, however, were achieved in no small part by removing low-income, "undesirable" residents from a given neighborhood.

TROUBLING PARTICIPATION IN URBAN AND ECONOMIC DEVELOPMENT

HOPE VI was the programmatic lodestar in a neoliberal approach to reduce the state's burden to house the nation's poorest—a crucial aspect of which manifested in HOPE VI's federal mandate that residents "participate" in redevelopment processes. For HOPE VI, participation generally meant enlisting resident input and feedback on the needs of the communities targeted for redevelopment. While participatory action research and methods have long been featured in community work, HUD appropriated participation in two major ways. To begin with, HUD instituted a perfunctory participation. The department mandated that housing authorities enlist resident participation through methods like surveys, forums, meetings, committees, resident councils, workshops, and newsletters.

Such methods are standard participatory tools. Indeed, HUD required that public housing authorities consult with public housing residents in drafting their initial redevelopment proposals. These consultations ideally took the form of "a resident training session and several public meetings" (Vale 2019, 27). However, these requirements

> remained vague, so actual practices varied quite a bit. . . [and] participation could often be rather rushed and limited, especially if a local tenant organization had leaders who were not broadly supported or well engaged with the full range of constituencies in the development. (Vale 2019, 27)

In this fashion, participation often became non-participatory. HUD policies created a crowding-out effect that ultimately amounted to something more akin to collusion among more powerful stakeholders. Likewise, HOPE VI embraced an oppositional stance in which these planning engagements served to manage the risk of resident pushback and stakeholder conflict, all while HUD used participatory rhetorics to legitimate its programs and to engage in selective inclusion and exclusion of resident input.

Second, HUD did not codify participatory requirements into law, which prevented any enforcement mechanism for residents to effectively implement their recommendations or to address their concerns, even as housing authorities went through the motions of community meetings, for example, to fulfill grant applications. The participation that HOPE VI brought about was a participatory arrangement that bolstered public-private partnerships more than it supported transformative community work. Moreover, the participation that HUD favored featured the enlistment of a wide range of institutions and organizations to support redevelopment. These organizations included but were not limited to local governments, developers, financiers, housing authorities, development associations, community organizations, architectural firms, and other private companies. This kind of participation was borne from the reduced direct role of the federal government in providing affordable housing. Accordingly, HUD was able to leverage rhetorics of participation to limit resident power, while at the same time empowering other organizations to fulfill the state's role to their own benefit.

Broadly, HOPE VI can be best characterized as an instance of participatory development, a development effort that acknowledges the benefits of working with local, "underdeveloped" communities. Though HOPE VI featured common participatory design methods like design workshops, HOPE VI was not a participatory design project. Additionally, though HUD and local housing authorities collaborated with residents to improve social services, HOPE VI was not an instance of participatory action research. Both of those approaches maintain standards and protocols that, as previously mentioned, were not institutionally, legally, or empirically stipulated in the HOPE VI program. HUD did, however, mandate that developers and local housing authorities enlist resident participation to some (though not entirely rigorous) effect to receive HOPE VI funding. That HUD's redevelopment efforts featured such a hodgepodge of methods with little coherence or accountability, however, illustrates a persistent operational and ethical problem with participation: it can devolve into an easy yet rhetorically powerful gesture that gives cover to institutional antagonism. Concerns about such perfunctory participation are not new. Many scholars have put forth typologies of participation, where, for instance, problematic participation takes the forms of "therapy" or "manipulation" and efficacious participation is defined by "citizens control" and "self-mobilization" (Larsen et al. 2015, 7). Such typologies are neither static nor simple. Rather, appeals to "citizenship" and "partnership"—the ethical end of the participatory spectrum—can facilitate a programmatic reality wherein the most vulnerable are manipulated and pathologized by institutional language. Qualifiers like "citizen" and "citizenship," for example, are often defined to implement processes of exclusion while they simultaneously presume to facilitate inclusion.

Participatory methodologies remain dubious tools for organizations seeking to enlist the expertise, input, and cooperation of marginalized communities, especially in contexts of housing, urban, and economic development. Methods like workshops, listening sessions, surveys, and public forums have long promised to reduce conflict between communities targeted for development on the one hand and organizations seeking to carry out development and interventional policies on the other. Yet, in many such contexts, disagreement, mistrust, and exploitation proliferate, prompting several scholars and practitioners to question the efficacy of participation. Participatory engagements often fall short of their democratic ideals because organizations and community members have divergent agendas. In numerous cases, organizations implement participatory projects in bad faith, using discourses and methods of participation with little to no institutional accountability for any outcome other than organizational control of a development or community project. Thus, what looks like organizational failure to effectively collaborate with communities can actually be an intended success in limiting resistance to institutional mandates at the expense of marginalized and vulnerable communities.

Contentious participatory projects often involve racialized and marginalized communities. Even those optimistic in their assessments of organizational uses of participation advise caution when appropriating participatory methods, because such projects can perpetuate the naturalization of racial difference and racialized hierarchies. Raelin (2012) notes that "Without authentic citizen voice, we risk having emancipatory discourse represent no more than a staged affectation" (16). Lang (2023) laments "the multiplication of mechanisms whose aim is more to build acceptance for urban renewal projects . . . or to tame criticism rather than to engage in co-constructed public policies" (100). In "Participatory Methodologies for Intersectional Research in Organisations," Plowman (2016) emphasizes reflexivity as "essential to . . . understanding[s] of power and silences. Revealing the impact of gender and race is found in what is unsaid, as well as what is said" (2016, 39). Scholars such as these highlight the delicate boundary between collaboration and co-optation when it comes to community or development work between organizations and communities of color. Some critics go further, however, and view racialization as endemic to participatory projects because racialized difference and hierarchy (particularly in development contexts) are socially and discursively taken for granted.

In its worst iterations, organizations seize upon this taken-for-grantedness to frame marginalized communities as incapable of self-determination or agency and thus as unworthy of being treated as legitimate partners. Demsas (2022), for example, argues that participatory approaches increase racial disparities in U.S. housing development policy, writing, "Expanding opportunities for political participation failed to solve the problem of inequitable project distribution, because the fundamental problem wasn't lack of community input; it was a lack of political power among disadvantaged groups." The view that participation undermines the most vulnerable stakeholders is not new in assessing organizations' uses of participatory methodologies. Critics have long questioned the sincerity and effectiveness of organizations that advocate for participation (Cleaver 1999; Williams 2004). Yet, despite participation's questionable effectiveness, organizational and institutional reliance on participatory methodologies remains. As Lee (2015) notes, "Participation is so normalized in the ideologies of contemporary organizations as to require new perspectives on participation, encompassing cross-cutting and overlapping discourses and practices experienced by participants as they move through the various organizations and communities in their lives" (2015, 279). Participation's persistence therefore poses the question: how have researchers, organizers, and policymakers (and, indeed, vulnerable stakeholders like the residents affected by HOPE VI) become captured by participation?

To begin answering this question, I present this book as a historical case study of the discursive and programmatic iterations of participatory capture in

HOPE VI. I use the term "participatory capture" to refer to the ways institutions and organizations engaged in participatory projects deploy participatory methods, however unintended, in ways that further endanger or disempower the most vulnerable participants. Participatory methodology was central to HOPE VI's implementation. Over the life of the program, policymakers

> emphasized the importance of resident participation in redevelopment efforts, especially in the planning of community and supportive services . . . [and] the redevelopment process. However, in actual practice, the rights of residents and others to participate in the HOPE VI process [were] much more limited than HUD's policies [suggested]. (National Housing Law Project 2002, 17)

Moreover, these limited policies negatively and disproportionately affected low-income, Black residents, many of whom were geographically and economically displaced because of HOPE VI. Yet, an often-overlooked aspect of HOPE VI's inequitable methods is the rhetoric, technical communication, and organizational discourse that facilitated its participatory policies. Ultimately, these policies in their participatory capture gave cover to institutional and organizational practices that actually limited resident participation and constrained residents' choices of where to live.

In the case of HOPE VI, participatory capture and its attendant organizational discourses reflected the logics of racial capitalism. Not surprisingly, households headed by Black women with children were disproportionately displaced—"not only in comparison to the US population as a whole, but also in comparison to the general public housing population" (Duryea 2006, 579). In light of the racial and economic disparities enacted by HOPE VI, and in further articulating participatory capture from a historical standpoint, I take the view that participatory appeals and policies "[leave] unexamined the cumulative economic effects of colonial power, that is, of the still-working mechanisms of dispossession, displacement, and death that facilitate the expropriation of the productive capacity of the lands and bodies of the 'others of Europe'" (Silva 2015, 35). In other words, institutionalized and organizational deployments of participation have the potential to obscure the power dynamics inherent in racialization and its reliance upon marginalized Others. Ndubuizu (2023) articulates similar linkages between the deployment of antiblack rhetoric and government housing policy, with what she calls *disciplinary housing governance*. She defines disciplinary housing governance as "the racially gendered and hegemonic ideology that draws on negative stereotypes about low-wage Black families to validate state-sponsored efforts to tie low-wage Black families' access to improved housing to the evaluation or surveillance of their domestic lives" (Ndubuizu 2023, 169). From that perspective, the racial and economic implications of HOPE VI lead me to ask, what subtle (and not-so-subtle) but effective discourse strategies and organizational models are at work when institutions advocate for participation in development contexts that are structurally constituted by racialized, gendered, and economic hierarchies?

Beyond the contemporary considerations of race and participation mentioned above, such a question prompts additional reconsiderations of the practical and ethical implications of race and participatory methodologies within management and organization studies. Sparre (2020) uses participatory action research, for instance, to support organizational learning but offers that "Who participates, how they participate, when they participate, and why they participate are questions that expose real differences" (2020, 5). Likewise, Gronouwe et al. (2021) advocate for a "participatory (re)design process which focusses on increasing the ability to self-design of employees" in integral organizational renewal (2021, 40). They concede, however, that "Yet, as a fully participative, bottom-up and non-directive redesign process is considered as unfeasible . . . it remains exposed to the possibility of expert-driven elements getting the upper hand, potentially nullifying its emancipatory potential" (Gronouwe et al. 2021, 40). Importantly, though, Puri and Sahay (2003) have intervened in organization studies with their examination of participatory methodology along the lines of ethnicity and nationality. They conclude that participatory methodology is mostly

> mediated by governmental agencies, drawing upon institutional structures that emphasize hierarchy, a top-down philosophy, and the application of a project-based scientific knowledge . . . [which] tend to stifle participatory processes, or at best accept inputs from the end-users within the development framework defined by the bureaucracy. (2003, 284)

I present a critical-cultural intervention like those of Puri and Sahay (2003) by articulating the discursive machinations of participatory capture. I argue that participatory methodologies and their relation to participatory capture complicate organizational and technical communication deployments of participation, especially in contexts wherein those enlisted to participate occupy sociocultural, ontological, and material positions of marginalization. In HOPE VI, for example, the U.S. federal government mandated the participation of low-income Black residents in ways that ultimately undermined the abilities of Black residents to effectively influence the development process.

Race and marginalization are central to evaluations and uses of participation, which has origins as a workplace approach to diversity. Indeed, participation has functioned as a methodological and communicative framework for negotiating classed and racialized difference. Participatory design, for instance, is rooted in workplace democracy movements in 1970s Europe, while participatory action research can be traced to decolonial labor movements also of the 1960s and 1970s (Robertson & Simonsen 2013; Lenette 2022). Today, participatory methods remain prevalent tools for engaging marginalized communities on behalf of institutions and organizations. In healthcare, for example, many practitioners rely on participatory communication for increasing public engagement in medical interventions in underserved communities (McFarlane et al. 2022; Seifer et al. 2010). Meanwhile, governments and local organizations have implemented processes like participatory budgeting, as ways to increase input from marginalized and racialized groups (Lerner & Secondo 2012; Kasdan et al. 2014). Technical communication researchers have long turned to participatory methodologies to coordinate varieties of stakeholders (Evia & Patriarca 2012; Moore & Elliott 2015). The social justice turn in technical communication values participation as a promising framework for bringing about diversity, equity, and inclusion (Agboka 2013; Moore 2018). Proponents of participation have legitimated its uses—that is, following sociologist Jürgen Habermas's concept of legitimation, sought to instill confidence in the administrative effectiveness of participation—by claiming that such methodologies instantiate democratic principles (Björgvinsson et al. 2012). Participation, however, has not been without its faults. Despite their often-purported social justice aims, participatory methodologies are fraught with racialized rhetorical and programmatic undercurrents that challenge the liberatory efficacy of the programs that participation supports.

This book (however related) is not a book explicitly about urban planning, public policy, economic development, or political science. My primary intervention is in rhetorical theory as applied to and practiced in technical and organizational communication. Thus, I offer critical discourse analyses of major technical communication texts—reports, manuals, and newsletters—associated with HOPE VI, particularly its community-building program which articulated its participatory methodology. My analysis of these documents further interrogates the racial and neoliberal assumptions of participatory discourse that are used uncritically in racialized and predatory development contexts. Economic development projects and policies tend to elide racialized power dynamics with rhetorical appeals to "markets," "democracy," and "progress," and yet such development projects often burden marginalized communities with unpayable debt, all while blaming racialized Others when markets, democracy, and progress stall or never materialize (Chakravartty & Silva 2012, 362). HOPE VI is an effective case study for understanding these dynamics because the program sits at the intersections of race, materialism, and identity, as well as institutional and organizational discourse, providing a productive lens with which to evaluate an instance of participatory capture, an analysis that offers discourses and methods to avoid in breaking free from (or at least better accounting for) the constraints of participation.

Some critics have indeed framed participation as a neoliberal rhetoric that builds consensus for economic development at the expense of the least powerful (Kaethler et al. 2017; Dore 2022). From the standpoint of racial and ethnic diversity, other critics further contend that participatory methodologies often ascribe vulnerability and dysfunction to people of color as immutable characteristics. Pin (2020), for instance, in a critical assessment of participatory budgeting, concludes that, "Consistent with a racial-deficits model of organizing, people involved in participatory budgeting presented certain racial groups as embodying attributes that made engagement in the process challenging" (2020, 587). Fashioning marginalized participants as vulnerable and pathological are persistent features of many participatory projects. Such persistence prompts the question, "How do organizations mobilize conceptions of diversity and participation to navigate racial and cultural difference in public engagement?" Quick and Feldman (2011) argue that "participation and inclusion are different and complementary ways of engaging diverse populations," with participation referring to programs, policies, and methods of community involvement, and inclusion referring to processes by which communities are formed (2011, 285). However, one area in need of further analysis is how participatory rhetoric functions as an essential communicative technology for "creating" the communities to be included and enlisted in public input. In other words, participation and inclusion are not necessarily separate processes. Rather, I argue, they work together in otherizing those called upon to participate. This otherizing tendency suggests that diversity as a concept relies on a racialized, participatory approach that allows institutions to engage in selective inclusion exemplifying how participatory rhetoric and methods tend to further legitimize the hierarchal difference it seeks to confront (i.e., how participatory rhetoric and methods capture their subjects).

DEFINING PARTICIPATORY CAPTURE

"Capture" or "regulatory capture," as terms in economics and political science, refer to the process whereby special interests overtake the capacity for public oversight and regulation in favor of monopolies or other self-interested motives (Laffont & Tirole 1991). The concept is applied in organization and management studies to refer to ways that organizations influence policies or processes in conflict with public resistance. In this view, organizations influence communities or stakeholders in order to reduce resistance to institutional goals. Importantly, capture is an exercise in power; capturers seek to gain or to consolidate power at the expense of collaboration, deliberation, and contestation by those most affected and who tend to be less powerful.

Along these lines, critics of participation have highlighted how participatory methodologies are prone to "elite capture," in which "communities are stratified along lines of wealth, class, ethnicity, gender, political affiliation, livelihood strategy, religion, and/or norms, and that elites within them tend to capture participatory initiatives for their own benefit and at the expense of non-elites" (Lund & Saito-Jensen 2013, 104). Critics of elite capture view participation with skepticism and argue that participation can

> reproduce and reinforce relations of domination and subordination between elites and non-elites, leaving little, if any, possibility for participatory initiatives to circumvent them, despite specific measures to prevent elite capture, such as regulations ensuring the representation of minority groups in decision-making forums. (Lund & Saito-Jensen 2013, 105)

Those who see capture as a persistent underlying dynamic within participatory initiatives refer to such dynamics as "participatory capture."

Historically, the term "participatory capture" has been deployed in two contexts. The first is a critique of participation in economic development. Young and Meijaard (2002) frame participatory approaches as a particularly Eurocentric mode of governance based on the assumption that "cultural predispositions are directly related to the manifestation of political culture and economic structure" (2022, 305). In northern Europe, for instance, political systems are based on consent and thus promote outcomes as states of "participatory capture," in which "regulatory capture is reversed" and "Agents are captured to commit themselves to accept the finally resulting social welfare" (Young & Meijaard 2002, 306). The second context in which participatory capture has been articulated is information systems development. Yu (2010) used the term to highlight "the gap between the theory of user participation and the user's lack of real influence on design and development" (2010, 185). Importantly, Yu reveals how user feedback can be co-opted by those with greater influence on a design project's communicative practices and also by participants' own reluctance or inability to effectively communicate resistance (2010, 193). Thus, participatory capture also refers to ways that participants lose or are deprived of critical perspective and independence even as their participation is used to legitimate a design project.

With respect to race and housing in the United States, Taylor (2019) articulates a similar phenomenon to participatory capture, which what she calls *predatory inclusion.* Predatory inclusion "describes how African American homebuyers were granted access to conventional real estate practices and mortgage financing, but on more expensive and comparatively unequal terms" (5). "Inclusion [in the American housing market] . . . would be conditional, contingent, and tiered," Taylor concludes, and "inclusion did not bring an end to predacious practices; it intensified them" (2019, 17). Likewise, in examining the persistence of racial segregation in Houston, Texas, Ponton (2024) deploys the term "capture" to reflect how Black residents are structurally constrained by racism. He writes that, for him, capture "refers to the various ways historical subjects, their actions, and their thoughts were always constrained by the worlds in which they lived: constricted by ideologies like gender and race, by faith in the law, and by hegemonic narratives" (2024, 4). My own articulation of participatory capture relies on similar critical traditions and assumptions, in that, in my argument, participatory capture becomes capture principally because it is a strategy conceived and executed amid structural hierarchy. Indeed, participation is meant to elaborate hierarchy in ways that legitimate institutions in all their racial, economic, and sexual antagonisms. Furthermore, Ponton argues, "racial capture . . . implicates antiblackness as a violence that is constitutive of the modern world. . . . Antiblackness traps people who are marked as black into a stubborn antagonism with the world" (2024, 4). While Ponton is concerned with "Domestic racial terrorism, the racialized criminalization of space, processes of annexation and underbounding, and so on [that] helped concretize Housing's racial geography," I am interested in how antiblackness manifested in the rhetoric of HOPE VI as animated by its emphasis on participation, and how such rhetoric worked in organizational and technical communication to affect negative outcomes for low-income and Black residents.

On that front, participatory approaches in organizations often carry within them inherent contradictions, namely that the greater the institutional invocation of participation, the less agential participants become. Howcroft and Wilson (2003) examine the paradoxes of participation, while emphasizing "the conceptualization of systems design and implementation as a process of social contention and political, as well as technical, determination" (2003, 2). The contention, which Howcroft and Wilson additionally term "fundamental antagonisms," arises since participation is typically deployed to mediate conflict between managers and end-users, institutions and agents. As such, a key aim of their argument is "highlighting the dissonance between rhetorics of participation and empowerment as against the actuality of maintenance of the relationship of power and powerlessness" (Howcroft & Wilson 2003, 3). Primarily, participation fails to reflect the actual dynamics at work in a systems design or public engagement effort. On one hand, the labor and rhetoric recognized as performed by participants do not necessarily represent what participants actually feel, think, or even contribute. On the other hand, participatory engagements often fail to accurately reflect the motivations and influences—institutional, local, personal, or otherwise—that animate such engagements. With my case study of HOPE VI, I illustrate how fundamental antagonisms between housing residents and governmental organizations lead to participatory capture.

Similarly, Rigg (2016) criticizes participation for not accounting for the power dynamics and political abuses inherent in development contexts, writing that proponents of participation do not "use the words 'politics' or 'political'" and that "participatory approaches are far from being politics-proof" (i.e., exempt from the cultural, social, and material forces that maintain structural inequality) (2016, 201). As a result, in lamenting the prevalence of participatory capture, Rigg (2016) asks two fundamental questions of participation: (1) "Are local systems of management socially inclusive and equitable with respect for example to women and ethnic minorities?" and (2) "Do participatory development initiatives tend to become captured and controlled by local elites for their own benefit?" (222). He concludes that participatory development is too conceptually aligned with civil society, which he says, "has its roots in Western thinking and experience" and likewise its methodological progeny of participation "conceals the power relations that are always present, in every society" (Rigg 2016, 222). My analysis of HOPE VI's technical communication builds on this perspective and further articulates participatory capture by showing how participation often legitimates longstanding social hierarchies even while such efforts make discursive claims to the contrary.

COMMUNITY BUILDING, RHETORIC, AND TECHNICAL COMMUNICATION IN HOPE VI

Participation was a major component of HOPE VI's community-building approach, which stipulated and regulated input from communities targeted for redevelopment. In fact, community building relied upon "the participation of both public housing residents living at HOPE VI sites awaiting revitalization and the surrounding community." The U.S. Department of Housing and Urban Development said, "The spirit of HOPE VI is one of consultation and collaboration among the housing authority, affected residents, social service providers, and the broader community" (HUD 2000, 1). Moreover, HOPE VI was "founded on four principles regarding the involvement of residents affected by demolition and new construction: collaboration, inclusion, communication, and participation. These principles also form a guide to resident participation outside the HOPE VI context" (HUD 2000, 67). HUD additionally remarked that

> Ideally, the housing authority and residents will be able to come together and develop a common vision. Residents must be invited to work closely with the

> housing authority in all phases of HOPE VI—from preparation of the application and planning through implementation and operation of the revitalized housing community. (HUD 2000, 67)

This "working closely" implies that residents maintained a direct influence on the process.

To that effect, organizational rhetoric and communication were integral to HOPE VI's participatory approach. Housing authorities were charged with "communicating with and disseminating information to all affected residents and ensuring that all affected residents have opportunities to participate in the activities related to the HOPE VI planning and development process" (HUD 2000, 67). Similarly, resident councils practiced constitutive rhetoric—the communicative act of identifying with groups of people—in aligning themselves with institutional processes. According to one HOPE VI manual *Community Building Makes a Difference* (2000),

> Resident councils must see themselves as representatives of the public housing community at large, keep the other residents informed of developments, and bring their concerns to the housing authority . . . ways must be found to represent the interests and concerns of non-public housing residents. (HUD 2000, 67)

From the perspective of non-resident stakeholders, communication was central to persuading residents, increasing identification, and informing the development process. Housing authorities were encouraged to "develop a public information strategy that provides for regular communication and information sharing with the residents regarding all aspects of the revitalization plan" (HUD 2000, 67). HUD mentioned that

> It may be necessary to simplify or explain certain technical concepts and to use translators in cases where English is not spoken. Some housing authorities have found that a regular HOPE VI newsletter is an effective means of keeping residents (especially those who are temporarily relocated) updated and connected to the revitalization process. (HUD 2000, 67)

Indeed, HUD's community building encompassed a variety of technical and professional communication applications, especially with respect to resident participation.

In HOPE VI, participants were additionally charged with procedural responsibilities related to organizational communication and project management. *Community Building Makes a Difference* offered that "Public housing developments that become [redeveloped] communities will present special concerns in such areas as representation, community strategizing, and establishing new priorities for action" (HUD 2000, 67). One example included a directive that "Residents should be encouraged to participate in the planning and implementation of the entire process." These planning and implementation activities included: "sitting on the selection panels that choose development partners and consultants; attending meetings with the development team, program manager, public and private lenders, the city, and other partners; and taking an active role in working or advisory groups" (HUD 2000, 67). At the same time, residents were presumed to suffer from a certain degree of unfamiliarity regarding the overall development process. HUD wrote, "To ensure their meaningful participation, the housing authority must provide training (generally through community partners) to residents on the fundamentals of technical development issues." Additionally, housing authorities were told to work with residents "to identify specific needs and appropriate sources of training to meet those needs" (HUD 2000, 67). In these scenarios, the residents were necessary though not entirely needed, functional though not agential. This assumption of ignorance as well as the utility of participant "ignorance" as necessary for meeting organizational goals reflects elements of HOPE VI's participatory capture, since the housing developments-to-be were not primarily resident-driven. Instead, HOPE VI's participatory approach served to limit resident input while relying on racialized tropes to legitimate the discursive and organizational structures of capture.

USING CRITICAL DISCOURSE ANALYSIS AND RHETORICAL CRITICISM TO READ HOPE VI

With implications for designers, researchers, advocates, and instructors, the purpose of this book is to interrogate the rhetorical and discursive machinations by which participation can be co-opted for institutional selectivity rather than for transformative outcomes. HOPE VI discriminated against its most vulnerable participants. To examine the relationship between the discrimination and the uses of participatory rhetoric, I apply rhetorical criticism and critical discourse analysis to reports, manuals, and newsletters associated with the HOPE VI program.

While discourse analysis argues that institutions are driven by ideologies, the rhetorical criticism I practice shows how such ideologies are reflected in language and lines of argument. I use critical discourse analysis (CDA) to show how the discourse of participation, with respect to HOPE VI, facilitated institutionalist goals in national housing policy. CDA is effective because it allows researchers to incorporate multiple theoretical perspectives, analyze a wide variety of texts and contexts, and identify patterns of presumptions in communication. Along these lines, CDA functions as a critically productive analytic tool by which to establish generic qualities of institutional communication practices by organizing "strategies" and "discourses." Additionally, CDA helps establish rhetorics of participation as I discuss them in this project, enabling me to explain how social realities are produced and maintained through language or the "ideological character of discourse" (Fairclough 2012, 10).

CDA is generally a recursive process of reading, whereby the practitioner moves interactively between theory and data collection. This process typically entails four stages: (1) identify a "social wrong" that has come about in a dialectical relationship between semiosis and event; (2) describe how ideology or other social elements take the semiotic aspect of the social wrong for granted such that there is a barrier to addressing the wrong; (3) consider how the social wrong constitutes the function of ideology or social relations; and (4) suggest "possibilities within the existing social process for overcoming obstacles to addressing the social wrong in question" (Fairclough 2012, 15). The "taking for granted" in the second analytic establishes compatibility with rhetorical criticism.

To evaluate institutional logics and their vocabularies, I practice rhetorical criticism on the artifacts—a total of thirteen HUD reports and archival documents, as well as thirty-eight newsletter articles. The rhetorical criticism I employ consists of the standard research process of selecting and analyzing artifacts, deriving research questions, reviewing literature, and theorizing communicative meaning therein. However, I take a more defined approach by engaging in ideological criticism, in which the critic "looks beyond the surface structure of an artifact to discover the beliefs, values, and assumptions it suggests" (Foss 2018, 237). In that respect, I perform the four analytical moves put forth by Foss (2018): "(1) identifying the presented elements of the artifact; (2) identifying the suggested elements linked to the presented elements; (3) formulating an ideology; and (4) identifying the functions served by the ideology" (2018, 243). This style of rhetorical analysis provides practitioners and scholars alike useful tools for explicating the complexity that lies at the heart of many social problems and solutions, while examining the relationship between rhetoric and methodology. This relationship is based on the idea that a document's rhetoric represents the communicative predicates and strategies involved in carrying out methodological practices. This relationship is ultimately how I establish links between HOPE VI's rhetoric, methods, and exclusionary effects.

CDA functions as a productive methodology by which to articulate characteristics of organizational discourse defined as

> the structured collections of texts embodied in the practices of talking and writing (as well as a wide variety of visual representations and cultural artifacts)

> that bring organizationally related objects into being as these texts are produced, disseminated and consumed. (Grant et al. 2004, 3)

The purpose of CDA is to bring to light "critically social inequality as it is expressed, constituted, legitimized, and so on, by language use (or in discourse)" (Wodak & Meyer 2009, 10). Additionally, critical discourse analysts argue that, given "new transnational, global and local developments and related institutions. . . phenomena such as 'depoliticization' and 'participation' need to be investigated in detail" (Wodak & Meyer 2009, 11). In practical terms, in dealing with larger theoretical concepts, CDA is "similar to Grounded Theory" in that

> data collection is not considered to be a specific phase that must be completed before analysis begins: after the first collection exercise, it is a matter of carrying out the first analyses, finding indicators for particular concepts, expanding concepts into categories and, on the basis of these results, collecting further data (theoretical sampling). (Wodak & Meyer 2009, 27–28)

In other words, critical discourse analysts read organizational texts for shared or comparative themes, representations, and rhetorical strategies.

I analyze HOPE VI organizational texts for discourse strategies related to participation, which, for the sake of this project, reflect linguist Ruth Wodak's discourse-historical approach, namely her discursive strategies of: referential/nomination, predication, and argumentation. Wodak (2001) defines the strategies of referential/nomination as "Construction of ingroups and out-groups" featuring "membership categorization, biological" and "naturalizing and depersonalizing metaphors and metonymies" (2001, 73). Predication is defined as "Labelling social actors more or less positively or negatively, deprecatorily or appreciatively" (Wodak 2001, 73). This strategy uses devices such as "stereotypical, evaluative attributions of negative or positive traits" and "implicit and explicit predicates" (Wodak 2001, 73). Finally, Wodak defines argumentation as "justification of positive or negative attributions," which relies upon "topoi used to justify political inclusion or exclusion, discrimination or preferential treatment" (Wodak 2001, 73). I identify these strategies in the HOPE VI materials because they are discursively attuned to the communicative predicates that facilitate participatory capture (i.e., how an organization's communication rhetorically constructs a participatory process with the effect of legitimizing hierarchy and exclusion). In this case, the participatory capture enacted by HOPE VI relied upon community-building processes and procedures as detailed in its technical communication documents, which I read and coded for Wodak's discourse-historical strategies mentioned above. Taken together, my methodological blend of critical discourse analysis and rhetorical criticism allowed me to scaffold reflexively between rhetorical characteristics at the sentence level, discursive characteristics within the ideological intent of the language, and the larger ideology animating the structure of HUD's communicative schema. In this way, my methodology is both grounded and deductive, each aspect informing the other as I articulate participatory capture in the particular instance of HOPE VI while also extrapolating its broader theoretical implications. This approach best aligns with technical communication's cultural studies turn and social justice turns, which I'll discuss and explain next, notably where I agree and disagree with each.

FROM HYPERPRAGMATISM TO CULTURAL STUDIES TO SOCIAL JUSTICE IN TECHNICAL COMMUNICATION

It should come as no surprise to technical and professional communicators that institutions co-opt potentially transformative or confrontational rhetorics. Though technical communication is currently undergoing a social justice turn, a "hyperpragmatist" approach historically has characterized the field, wherein students, researchers, and practitioners have worked primarily on behalf of institutions. Over the past two decades, however, scholars have sought more effective methods for addressing those affected by institutions, especially marginalized communities and vulnerable populations. Today, many technical communicators prioritize research that both empowers community members and supports democratic entities, as a way toward shedding the hyperpragmatist label, redefining what it means to be a technical communicator, and as a way toward enriching the sustainability of the field. In this regard, the goal of my research is to expand the theoretical and methodological considerations of today's social turn by integrating a critical-qualitative studies approach and by promoting greater efficacy as it relates to the budding relationship between culture, research, and practice within technical and professional communication.

Technical communication can be understood as "the means by which institutions define themselves and conduct their cultural work" (Britt 2006, 148). Moreover, technical communication's defining research question is: "How do texts . . . and related communication practices mediate knowledge, values, and action in a variety of social and professional contexts?" (Rude 2009, 176). Accordingly, much of the field concerns itself with understanding the means by which institutions affect outcomes—both intended and unintended—as a result of communication practices. Along these lines, a historicization of technical writing instruction within the academy reveals that, early on, American professional culture viewed technical writing as "hyperpragmatist"—something taught for the primary purpose of serviceable workplace communication. In fact, throughout the initial decades of English Departments, "technical writing" was synonymous with "engineering writing" (Slack et al. 1993, 29).

This pragmatic view set the stage for technical writers' transparency; meaning that professional writers were expected to do the work of the institution and transmit institutional messages in a particular way such that writers, institutions, and their products were indistinguishable. In this scenario, not only is the writer rendered in service to the institution, but instructors—with all their pressures to prepare students for the "real world"—are also rendered in service. Meanwhile, both readers and consumers are forced to take the institution at face value, further iterating the need for critical approaches as a way of maintaining accountability and addressing manifestations of power. With these manifestations in mind, trust within the field is a contentious issue. Critiques developed in response to "the rupture in public trust by technical communication mobilized more for profit and greed than the public good . . . [like] tobacco and pharmaceutical marketing, finance and accounting reports, [and] energy regulatory standards" (Ornatowkski & Bekins 2004, 252). Toward these critical ends, scholars in the 1980s and 1990s turned to cultural studies and laid the foundation for a host of critiques and methodologies aimed at ethics rather than transparency.

The field's cultural turn marked a shift in research from an institution-oriented focus to a community- or user-oriented focus. Scholars began to prioritize balance and collaboration rather than top-down approaches that perpetuated practitioner transparency and community erasure. Within the cultural turn, technical communication became concerned with "questions about identity [and how] questions on power might shift their focus . . . from disciplinary problems to using . . . knowledge about texts and related communication practices to help solve social, educational, and organizational problems" (Rude 2009, 192–193). In this regard, scholars considered research to be an experience that ought to empower the individual's democratic and critical capacities to interpret power.

Longo (2006), for instance, asserted that "because technical writing knowledge is made through institutions such as schools and publishing companies, naive or uneducated technical writing practices are organized through academic and economic systems, which tend to reproduce our culture's dominant scientific model" (2006, 117). Longo concluded that culturally attuned discursive analyses "can illuminate how struggles for knowledge legitimation taking place within technical writing practices are influenced by institutional, political, economic, and/or social relationships, pressures, and tensions within cultural contexts that transcend any one affiliated group" (Longo 2006,

120). As such, examining the larger effects of technical communication—its practices and products—remains a central value.

Culturalists in technical communication study what happens both inside and outside of a particular organization or context in relation to an organization's texts. In this way, the cultural approach inspired a genre approach to understanding how organizations produce and reflect knowledge—an approach that gestures toward myriad actors and diverse ways of knowing that check institutional abuses and empower participants. Here, genre refers to "forms of cultural knowledge" and how they manifest in particular situations. Additionally, genre seeks to address

> knowledge of what and whose purposes genres serve; how to negotiate one's intentions in relation to genres' social expectations and motives; when and why and where to use genres; what reader/writer relationships genres maintain; and how genres relate to other genres in the coordination of social life. (Barwashi & Reiff 2010, 4)

The development of genre studies is important because it provided methods to study cultures as discrete but interactive. Indeed, today's social turn has followed the cultural turn, in which genre studies proliferate.

While interrogations of power influenced the field during the period of the late-1980s to the mid-2000s, in much of the past decade, some scholars have sought additional ways to bring about remedies to systemic abuses and imbalances. Along such lines, social justice theories and social justice methodologies have emerged in the hopes of activating cultural criticism for real-world change. The field has become increasingly defined by methodological reform bolstered by expanding theoretical frontiers, particularly with respect to race and community. As such, social justice approaches in technical communication contend that

> reconsidering research . . . practices is a grassroots way for integrating considerations of diversity (a focus on the inclusion of varied perspectives and viewpoints) and social justice (critical reflection and action that promotes agency for the marginalized and disempowered) into [technical and professional communication] . . . scholarship. (Jones 2016, 343)

This symbiosis between diversity (theory) and justice (action) defines much of the social justice approach.

Diversity, in this instance, is marked by a theoretical orientation away from mainstream, hegemonic, or purely institutional gaze. Moreover, diversity denotes a newfound concern for race and ethnicity in the field, since "Despite [the] promise of cultural studies work in technical communication, only a few scholars within our field are doing work specifically and explicitly at the intersections of race, ethnicity, rhetoric, and technology studies" (Haas 2012, 281). Action, on the other hand, is near-synonymous with participatory design in the broadest sense, because of its emphasis on communities in question rather than on exclusively institutional aims. Participatory design is a research methodology in which users or communities work with designers and technical communicators to produce texts or outcomes. This methodology developed alongside the cultural approach, as a way of legitimating the knowledge of localized communities within the process of accomplishing institutional goals. Social justice researchers aim to reform participatory or user-based research in order to overcome persistent power imbalances such as the "victimhood trope," which "ultimately leads to a paternalistic relationship between designers and workers" (Spinuzzi 2003, 10).

When it comes to diversity, Haas (2012) has worked to undo the cultural and racial erasure that undergirds technical communication. She indicates that

> technical communication . . . has a history of ignoring the ways in which our work is saturated with white male culture—which has real effects related to privilege and oppression on the lives and work of designers, writers, editors, and audiences of technical communication. (2012, 284)

Considering the field's intimate association with Western corporate and academic cultures, the attendant, exploitative erasure of racism and of communities of color comes as no surprise. As a result, scholars have looked to bring about "an antenarrative [that] allows the work of the field to be reseen, forges new paths forward, and emboldens the field's objectives to unabashedly embrace social justice and inclusivity as part of its core (rather than marginal or optional) narrative" (Jones et al. 2016, 212). Critical race studies and decolonial methodologies are two essential theoretical approaches to this antenarrative. Within the context of technical communication, Jones (2016) argues that critical race studies "allows researchers . . . to deconstruct how texts are used to empower or further oppress certain racial groups" (2016, 352). In this regard, critical race studies take the form of materialist and discursive interrogations. Decolonial perspectives, meanwhile, hold that ways of knowing and of communicating vary across culture and location. Additionally, decolonial scholars concern themselves with highlighting hegemonic abuses—discursive and otherwise—toward the end of overturning power imbalances inspired by colonial practices. Haas argues that decolonial approaches

> (a) redress colonial influences on perceptions of people, literacy, language, culture, and community and the relationships therein and (b) support the coexistence of cultures, languages, literacies, memories, histories, places, and

> spaces—and encourage respectful and reciprocal dialogue between and across them. (2012, 297)

Flowing from the concern for coexistence, equality, and diversity, participatory design and participatory action research (and user experience relatedly) remain principal research methods promoted by the social justice approach.

On the one hand, participatory research is the methodological offspring of the concept of genre, which punctuates the cultural approach, since "Genre is a sort of social memory that its practitioners accept without their explicit recognition that they are doing so" and "Communities, then, develop genres over time to mediate relatively stable, cyclical activities" (Spinuzzi 2003, 43, 48). On the other hand, today's scholars believe that participatory research facilitates dialogue and respect across and within various contexts, ranging from and including organizations, academia, and community. Participatory research—collaboration between technical communicators and users/communities—is "suitable for encouraging and supporting democratic ideals and creating change in local communities and beyond through the engagement in textual activism" (Jones 2016, 355). Finally, participatory methods are necessary to "sharpen the ability for [critical studies] to engage seriously the voices of marginalized rhetorical communities and mundane discourses that often evade critical attention[,]" . . . helping "to analyze situations in which meanings depend on places, physical structures, spatial delineations, interactive bodies, and in-the-moment choices" (Middleton et al. 2011, 387–388). In other words, participation helps to discover, to acknowledge, and to overcome differences. As a research method, however, participation has become institutional and should be evaluated as such—in line with a critical stance effectuated by cultural-critical scholars in technical communication.

In the disciplinary narrative of technical and professional communication, this book derives from the cultural studies approach that interrogates how organizations activate discourses. Importantly, cultural critics within the field concern themselves with how discourse at the institutional level produces genres and communication practices at the organizational level. In this regard, cultural studies scholars tend to differentiate organizations from institutions. Institutions are understood as ideological antecedents to social activity, such that institutions legitimate social life and its organization (Britt 2006; Porter et al. 2000). Britt (2006), for example, writes that "unlike formal organizations, which exhibit self-consciousness, institutions are marked by a certain taken-for-grantedness" (2006, 136). In other words, organizations are small instances of social behavior while institutions define behavior as socially acceptable or unacceptable.

Following advocacy that technical communication scholars conduct research with larger contexts in mind, culturally minded researchers prioritize "discourse as situated within institutions" and interrogate "how knowledge-making practices, ontological assumptions, and implicit values shape the reception or production of discourse . . . [and its] functions (rhetorically and materially) within and between institutions" (Britt 2006, 137). Longo, when she writes that "[r]ecognition of an organization's participation in cultural contexts enables a critical study that can illuminate assumptions about the inevitable roles of technical writing in our culture at given historical moments[,]" reflects and inspires a number of scholars past and present (113). Blyler (1998), for instance, calls for critical research in technical communication, wherein "researchers are deeply concerned about issues of ideology and power" (39). Earlier, Herndl (1993) decrees the fact "that [traditional professional writing] research describes the production of meaning but not the social, political, and economic sources of power which authorize this production or the cultural work such discourse performs" (222). Notably, around the same time, Slack et al. (1993) assert that the "technical communicator and technical discourse facilitate, sustain, generate, and disrupt relations of power" (163). From these perspectives, scholars like Scott, Grabill, Salvo, and indeed Longo continually critique views that saw technology, information, and knowledge as objective or inevitable. These authors concern themselves not so much with individual organizational studies, but rather with explanations of how certain forms of knowledge and language—even technical writing itself as a discipline—manifest in a world of material and cultural contention.

Numerous additional researchers have taken up the cause of situating technical writing within areas of study ranging from disability and gender to postcoloniality. Specifically, such contemporary scholars as Jones, Haas, and Agboka have prioritized inquiry that highlights power relations in technical communication along the lines of race and nationality. Importantly, Haas suggests that race is a constructive heuristic for understanding difference, especially since the category of "whiteness" relies upon an oppositional binary that views "non-white" as essentially different, while obscuring whiteness's own particularities. Accordingly, understanding structural antagonisms (i.e., binaries) serves to demystify privileged cultures (e.g., whiteness) not as objective or inevitable but as constructed and perpetuated (Haas 2012, 282–285). Along similar but also slightly different lines, Jones (2016) calls for an inclusive, social justice stance among researchers and practitioners. This stance works from a humanist perspective. Jones writes that, "technical communicators must be aware of the ways that the texts and technologies that they create and critique reinforce certain ideologies and question how communication shaped by certain ideologies affect individuals" (2016, 345). Jones and Haas are similar in that they both interrogate technical communication as an institution, while also relying upon familiar onto-epistemic frameworks like race and "humanity" to remediate the field's positivistic roots.

Agboka (2014) joins Jones's appeal for social justice approaches in technical communication research. He also reflects Haas's support for decolonial perspectives, writing that "current approaches, which are motivated by modernist ideologies and whose history is tied to the colonial project, may not be well-positioned to address emerging social justice challenges in many post-colonial, developing, and unenfranchised/disenfranchised cultural sites" (2014, 298). As a response to the traditional colonial character of the field, Agboka (2014) encourages research that makes "participants active collaborators in research projects by positioning them—not as subjects/objects, but as equal participants" (2014, 299). In this regard, a concern for participation and its efficacy as both a research methodology and as a communication strategy appears central to moving technical communication out of its intercultural morass. Agboka (2013) points toward "participatory localization" as a redemptive methodology for technical communication. Participatory localization is a user-centered design approach "undertaken from the ground up and 'in which human beings and their attendant physiological strengths and limitations are the center of technology design'" (2013, 42). This approach stands in contrast to traditional localization practices that tend to enact user-centered design from a set of criteria predetermined by firms and not by affected communities.

Participatory localization, on the other hand, relies on local situatedness from the inception of the design process. In other words, participatory localization demands that local culture determine function rather than merely inform it. This methodology stems from Agboka's question, "To what extent can we, technical communicators, account for social justice in international technical communication practices? Or, in what ways are we addressing issues of social justice in international contexts through our discursive practices?" (Agboka 2013, 28). Accordingly, participatory localization seems a logical development in technical communication's cultural studies. With this development in mind, I embrace the growing participatory ethos in technical communication. However, this book seeks to initiate a critical intervention in this area by highlighting the ways in which participation, as currently rendered, fails to upend structural antagonisms and how institutions and organizations appropriate the discourse of participation to maintain hierarchy.

With respect to the direction of the field, I argue that proposals heretofore from the social justice approach run the risk either of replicating power dynamics or of inadequately addressing power dynamics to start. I believe that the direction of social justice research may be derailed by conventional theories of diversity (and thus of participation), which seem to function as faulty compasses toward the efficacious empowerment of disenfranchised and marginalized communities. Specifically, I contend that a more radical union between rhetorical criticism and critical race studies is essential for achieving sustainable critical consciousness, especially with respect to participatory methodology. I especially worry about frameworks that fail to account for how: (1) the individual internalizes and thus reenacts conceptions of justice that were institutionally mediated to start; and (2) the dynamics of power among various individuals and groups that invariably facilitate replications of hierarchies, which institutions may not directly inspire but which they may certainly exploit or exacerbate. The potentially faulty assumption inherent in such a framework is that the individual, and indeed the technical communicator, is so potentially unique as to be devoid of ideology. Akin to a neoliberal model of diversity, this assumption may serve, in the end, to divest institutions (and individuals) of any social responsibility.

Moreover, I caution against deploying any similar bracketing of power relations from which notions of humanism and equality flow; meaning that even if the most individualistic, decolonial perspective were acknowledged, how would such an acknowledgment unto itself address both institutional and group preferences that may or may not ultimately reject or subjugate the perspective in question? It may be argued, then, that cosmopolitanism, for instance, is a form of power that elides hierarchical structures in much the same way as critical gestures toward equality. Both "equality" and "cosmopolitanism" as frameworks for addressing power favor (neo)liberal narratives of individual, productive uniqueness.

Accordingly, the critical intervention I'd like to make is to introduce a countertheory of diversity into technical communication. The theory I propose rejects the aforementioned flattened diversity as an ethical paradigm. Such rejection, I believe, is critical for escaping the persistent traps of transparency and victimhood sprung by deeply embedded allegiances to liberalism and neoliberalism that may continue to plague technical communication. Overall, neither communities nor individuals can ever undergo affirmation if their fundamental existences, their ontologies, continue to be subsumed by ideological mobilizations of categorical distinctions for market or institutional value. In other words, cultures and genres—even in their interactions with others—must be understood as distinct and whole, rather than as parts of a "humanity" that has never instantiated equality. Here, both equality and the human are ideological concepts that proliferated alongside the racism and colonization that these same concepts now claim to remedy. This paradox may indeed be resolved with a different critical approach. To that effect, I turn to the post-humanist critiques of Radical Black scholars like Frank B. Wilderson III and Saidiya V. Hartman, who argue that the way out of the paradox of liberalism is to more fully consider the perspectives and problems of Blackness.

Radical Black Studies are founded upon a critique of traditional cultural studies and humanism—both of which, scholars argue, obscure how the ontology of Blackness is constituted by a preclusion of efficacious Black participation in both humanity and traditional politics. In this regard, Radical Black scholars examine the ways in which Black subjectivity has become paradoxical—meaning that Blackness has typically been construed as inhuman, uncivil, and unproductive and thus highlights a structural paradigm wherein notions of culture, democracy, and the human have been weaponized against Black communities and non-hegemonic instances of "humanity," "production," and "culture." Here, Radical Blackness assails traditional cultural studies for bolstering a "paradigmatic explanation of relations" that continuously views Blackness through a cultural lens indelibly shaped by an ontology that purports the inhumanity of Blackness. Traditional cultural studies, then,

> insists on a grammar of suffering which assumes that we are all positioned essentially by way of the symbolic order . . . and as such our potential for stasis or change . . . is overdetermined by our "universal" ability or inability to seize and wield discursive weapons. (Wilderson 2010, 56)

The central critique, then, is of the "universality of the grammar of culture that modernity reified in its relation to and dependence on the African slave trade" (Wilderson 2010, 358). This rejection of the "universal" additionally constitutes the rejection of the human. With such a rejection in mind, Radical Black scholars "question whether the rights of man and citizen are realizable or whether the appellation 'human' can be borne equally by all" (Hartman 1997, 6). From that perspective, participation can be seen as a rhetorical and ideological constraint against those most adversely affected by the system calling upon them to participate.

This assessment follows from the narrative that, in addition to subjugating Blackness in the process of enslavement, the dominant ontological and cultural paradigms also fashioned the Black from utter abjection into an (un)civil creation (i.e., recognized or made human by the same institutions and logics that had obliterated Black subjectivity from the beginning). A Radical Black orientation is appropriate for an analysis of HOPE VI given its paradigmatic violence committed against low-income, Black, and woman participants. Given this imperative against the humanist, participatory impulse, I conclude this book by proposing sovereignty as the paradigmatic counter to participation. While participants are named and recruited by institutions, sovereignty is practiced by individuals and local communities. From that perspective, in this project, I define sovereignty as the networks, behaviors, forms of knowledge, and ways of life that community members have developed despite, irrespective of, or in response to institutionalism. Sovereignty, as I see it, is a stance against institutionalist power to determine the "right" courses of action.

Many scholars have similarly sought to reimagine sovereignty. Notably, in rhetorical studies, Lyons (2000) invokes a Native perspective and advocates for rhetorical sovereignty, which he defined as "the inherent right and ability of peoples to determine their own communicative needs and desires [and] to decide for themselves the goals, modes, styles, and languages of public discourse" (2000, 449–450). He adds that

> For indigenous people everywhere, sovereignty is an ideal principle, the beacon by which we seek the paths to agency and power and community renewal. Attacks on sovereignty are attacks on what it enables us to pursue; the pursuit of sovereignty is an attempt to revive not our past, but our possibilities. (Lyons 2000, 458)

Rhetorical sovereignty as defined by Lyons is a sort of anti-sovereignty as against that practiced by the State.

Broadly, I mobilize the concept of sovereignty as a rhetorical-design practice of possibility with awareness of Tiffany Lethabo King's argument that the positioning between Blackness and Native sovereignty is relational rather oppositional. She writes, "Black bodies in the fluttering, stretching, and changing states became a symbol of unstable borders, processes, and . . . shifting power relations" (King 2016, 1023). She continues, "Blackness, as expansion and spatial possibility, becomes a constituting feature of the spatial imagination of the conquistador/settler rather than just another human laborer exploited as a mere technology to produce space" (King 2016, 1023). In other words, antiblackness and settler colonialism are co-constitutive dynamics of subjugation. Likewise, Iyko Day (2015) has noted that "Expanding the scope beyond a black/Indigenous frame, we can explore how other groups have been subject to or have expressed different forms of economic irrationality in the context of settler colonialism" (2015, 116). With this perspective in mind, I view the problem of sovereignty as a generative space for redressing and resisting hegemonic, terroristic power.

Unlike participation, the sovereignty I advocate for does not seek to elide, perpetuate, or accede to power relations. Instead, from a communication standpoint, sovereignty is the naming of difference and the practice of identification by highlighting the lived resistances to power. After all, public housing residents' abilities to take ownership of redevelopment would always be refracted and defined by the sovereign state. But, to accept this reality as a given rather than as an iterative institutional arrangement is to abdicate ethical responsibilities as designers and communicators. Moreover, "Blackness marks and is marked by the Middle Passage and its aftermaths . . . also by black performativities that escape and re-mark that marking through the movement of difference" (Stormer 2019, 3). As such, a passive acceptance of institutionalism as given rather than architected is to reduce Black residents to instrumentalized units to be managed.

SUMMARIZING THE INTRODUCTION AND PREVIEWING THE NEXT CHAPTERS

The Introduction has presented the following key claims and interventions:

- HOPE VI was a U.S. federal housing program that, from about 1992–2012, facilitated the demolition of public housing units in favor of vouchers, urban redevelopment, and homeownership. This program was the capstone of the HOPE VI era, a three-decade period characterized by the dismantling of public and affordable housing, which has disproportionately affected Black and low-income residents.
- HOPE VI relied significantly on rhetorics, discourses, and methods of participation as ways of "including" Black and low-income residents in redevelopment. However, HOPE VI's participation served to divest vulnerable communities of input and influence.
- HOPE VI was an instance of participatory capture wherein institutions and organizations engaged in participatory projects deploy participatory methods, however unintended, in ways that further endanger or disempower the most vulnerable participants.
- Participatory capture suggests that participatory rhetorics and methodologies have the potential to reinforce racial, economic, and sexual hierarchies because hierarchy is built into participation's discursive invocations and methodological deployments.
- Participatory capture in HOPE VI has significant implications for rhetorical theory as well as for organizational and technical communication. HOPE VI not only implemented its agenda using technical and public writing genres like reports, manuals, and newsletters, but the program also used participatory rhetoric in its writing and methods in ways that complicate technical communication's social justice turn, which endorses participation as an ethical framework.
- Since participation is a troubled framework, a new technical communication ethics based on sovereignty has greater potential to account for and counteract how participation, diversity, and institutionalism often rely on antiblackness.

The following chapters elaborate on the aforementioned claims and interventions:

In chapter 2, I examine two federal reports associated with HOPE VI to establish how HUD's discourse and rhetoric of participation framed vulnerable Black participants. Moreover, I articulate four primary legitimation strategies that HUD used in its writing—legitimation strategies that demonstrate how participation is not a neutral term or a set of ideas.

Chapter 3 builds on this critique of neutrality to show that participation is not a neutral methodology. Chapter 3 features the analysis of HOPE VI manuals that detail the program's participatory approach to community engagement. Chapter 2 demonstrates connections between the program's rhetoric and the program's methods and shows how certain conceptions of participation limit democratic outcomes. While chapter 3 ultimately endorses community organizations, it presents two models of development wherein HUD rhetorically framed residents and organizations in ways that circumscribed local community agency.

In chapters 4 and 5, I analyze community newsletters written for HOPE VI's public housing residents. I explain the relevance of the newsletter genre to technical communication in community development, and I read the newsletters to demonstrate how HOPE VI's legitimation strategies proliferated within the newsletters' discourse. Chapter 5, however, serves as a potential starting point for exploring how technical communicators might more ethically support the mobilization of social networks and local cultures through the critical lens of sovereignty.

Chapter 6 concludes with implications for teaching and future research. Specifically, I conclude by offering a framework for reflexivity that students and teachers can use when engaging in community-based projects; strategies that technical communicators can use when implementing critical race theory; and, finally, a critical lens with which technical communicators and policy officials can evaluate dynamics of expertise in public engagement.

Chapter 2

Justifying "A New Era of Cooperation"

Participation, Diversity, and Legitimation in HOPE VI

On September 9, 1999, then-U.S. secretary of Housing and Urban Development, Andrew Cuomo, announced a $70 million grant to demolish aging public housing units in Newark, New Jersey. Joined by mayors, senators, and congressional representatives, Cuomo announced,

> We are transforming public housing projects with problems into new mixed-income communities with promise . . . We are making public housing a launching pad to opportunity, jobs and self-sufficiency—instead of a warehouse trapping people in poverty and long-term dependence. ("Cuomo Announces" 1999)

Cuomo and other political representatives spoke of "partnership" among housing and development stakeholders.

Among the sites to be demolished was the famed Stella Wright Homes, which hosted a four-year rent strike in the early 1970s—the longest in the nation's history. The strike, inspired by "mistrust that [had] characterized relationships between black tenant representatives and predominantly white administrators in the Newark Housing Authority," ended with a legal settlement that included federal funding as well as a "democratic" plan "that would both educate all of the tenants and give them power and responsibility over their own homes . . . [and] that would allow each resident to have a role through participation" (Cook 1975). This concern for participation reflected the social activism of the 1960s and 1970s, when activists and residents understood participation to mean transformative action directed primarily by those most affected. From that point on, participation became a major selling point in advocating for national housing reform.

Although the Department of Housing and Urban Development claimed that "full resident involvement and community participation are crucial elements of the HOPE VI Program" (National Housing Law Project 2002, 17), resident control was not prominent in Cuomo's appearance. Nor was resident control touted by the Clinton Administration, which instead emphasized, "broad-based partnerships to involve public housing residents, state and local government officials, the private sector, non-profit groups and the community at large in planning and implementing the new communities" ("Cuomo Announces" 1999). In fact, the Newark Housing Authority (NHA) outsourced the consequential grant application process to a consulting firm that specialized in social policy. The firm wrote that they

> worked closely with the NHA, residents, city officials, and key stakeholders to develop a HOPE VI plan that leveraged public and private funding to develop a $137 million mixed-income rental and homeownership community with new streets and utilities and two new community centers. ("1999 HOPE VI Application" 1999)

This conflation of participation and institutional coordination, however, signaled a new, neoliberal era of participation that prioritized development agendas rather than sovereign, communal visions.

It would take years before the Stella Wright Homes were eventually demolished, and by 2011, New Jersey had received over $400 million in HOPE VI grants, the most of any state (Malinconico 2011). The state, however, remained plagued by chronic homelessness, unaffordable housing, and overcrowding in public housing. Housing experts implicated HOPE VI, as the program did not mandate replacing the public housing it tore down. And, though housing authorities were required to submit appropriate relocation plans designed to help residents, they chose not to implement them. In the case of the Stella Wright Homes, "The housing authority . . . started eviction proceedings against many Stella Wright tenants before the relocation process began" (Malinconico 2011). The fate of the Stella Wright Homes and the chronic shortcomings of New Jersey's public housing illustrate participatory capture, namely three major problems with respect to how "participation" in HOPE VI aligned with institutional action that worked against its participants: (1) residents lived in a contentious relationship with the state's institutions, (2) the state used the rhetoric of participation to enlist a greater number of institutional stakeholders, and (3) the mixed-income development model undermined the goal of affordable housing.

The use of participatory rhetoric amid New Jersey's increased homelessness exemplifies how participation and appeals to resident involvement drew attention away from the ways in which institutions failed vulnerable residents. The concept of "participation" was central to HOPE VI's discourse and implementation. Over the life of the program, policymakers

> emphasized the importance of resident participation in redevelopment efforts, especially in the planning of community and supportive services . . . [and] the redevelopment process. However, in actual practice, the rights of residents and others to participate in the HOPE VI process [were] much more limited than HUD's policies [suggested]. (National Housing Law Project 2002, 17)

Yet, an often-overlooked aspect of HOPE VI's "participation" is the policy discourse that preceded, indeed constituted, participatory capture. That the discursive aspect of participation is overlooked is not incidental—institutions regularly deploy participatory discourses in efforts to reduce scrutiny and opposition. HOPE VI represents a neoliberal approach to housing policy and was "one of the centerpieces of the HUD reinvention [that exemplified] such core principles of neoliberal urbanization as entrepreneurialism and personal responsibility" (Jones & Popke 2010, 115). These principles were conflated in HOPE VI's participatory rhetoric and helped HUD avoid addressing systemic issues that continuously undermined racial and economic disparities in development politics. To further explore the relationship between the perpetuation of disparities and the use of participatory rhetoric, this chapter engages in a rhetorical criticism that may provide a starting point for interrogating the efficacy of liberal and neoliberal fault lines in technical and professional communication's social justice approach.

Importantly, the methods of participation are linked to the rhetorics and discourses of participation. W. Michele Simmons's *Participation and Power: Civic Discourse in Environmental Policy Decisions* (2007) is especially instructive for thinking through this relationship between language and methods when it comes to institutional engagement with publics. Simmons (2007) reveals how public participation policies implemented by the U.S. federal government "actually worked to prevent significant participation" (43). In her historical analysis of risk communication in environmental policy, she finds that the government's documentation and technical communication (via laws, regulations, and reports) mandated limiting the programmatic extent to which affected residents could be heard on policy matters (Simmons 2007, 64, 85–108). On this front, Simmons demonstrates that participation works at the levels of both language and policy, rhetoric and methods, since the language in the documentation prescribes programmatic methods. Simmons calls for a "rhetoric of ethical participation [that identifies] . . . the unequal power relations that currently work to marginalize public involvement" (2007, 18). Toward that end, my approach in this book is more proscriptive than prescriptive. I highlight communication practices to identify and to avoid. I seek to engage in a rhetoric of ethical participation by highlighting the rhetorical assumptions and strategies that HOPE VI, in instantiating participatory capture, used to co-opt participation, diversity, and inclusion.

I demonstrate that subsidized housing and mixed-income housing are products of a neoliberal ideology of diversity and reflect contemporary racialized population management. Diversity (i.e., racial difference) has become a commodity that development professionals sell to renters, buyers, and investors in a marketization of race. This marketization constructs racial (and other differentialized) representations as archetypal—by which I mean that diversity connotes a "desirable" form of racial difference that organizations, workplaces, and institutions operationalize through policy and rhetoric. Often, these diversity measures work against racialized subjects by obscuring how "desirable" forms of diversity legitimate institutional and structural violence against "undesirable" subjects. In U.S. housing, as privatization and pro-growth agendas took hold in the 1980s, federal support for low-income housing took the primary form of subsidies to "desirable" lower-income renters so that these renters could live in whiter, higher-income neighborhoods. Diversity, as a reflection of racialized desirability,

> indicated a shared buy-in into an unmarked white, middle-class culture of tolerance . . . made possible by selective inclusion—the incorporation of respectable people of color among white people—but threatened by overwhelming numbers of unrespectable, low-income minorities and the low-cost rental housing they depended upon. (Berry 2015, 150)

In the contemporary neoliberal housing market, even newer, "affordable" housing initiatives (funded by subsidies to private developers) relied on racial population management to maintain the "desirability" of redeveloped areas. The result of these policies was that those most in need of affordable housing were often excluded from economic gain, further entrenching systemic inequality.

Frequently, diversity means symbolically flattening difference even as such difference is explicitly represented. Such flattening stipulates the insufficient (un)critical frameworks of equality and cosmopolitanism (i.e., diversity) discussed in the previous chapter. In deploying those frameworks, what communication practitioners often miss is how difference is constructed such that institutions, organizations, and workplaces can go about the business of erasure. Importantly, participatory methodologies and their communication functioned as key rhetorical tools for the articulation of undesirability. HOPE VI illustrates the rhetorical strategies by which institutions actually construct undesirable subjects to legitimate their own visions for a desirable diversity.

The following documents were chosen for analysis, based on their significance in the federal deliberation processes that legitimated HOPE VI as policy:

- *A Decent Place to Live*—a seventy-one-page report completed in March 1988 by the National Housing Task Force, which the report says, "was established in September 1987, as part of a Congressional effort to reexamine America's housing policy" (HUD 1988, para. 1). The report states that the purpose of the Task Force was "to undertake a comprehensive review of housing policy" (HUD 1988, para. 3). Moreover, the Task Force was comprised mostly of developers, including James Rouse, a pioneer of urban renewal—or "Negro Removal" as James Baldwin once remarked—but also included financiers David O. Maxwell and Lewis Ranieri, who would both later be criticized for their roles in the subprime mortgage crisis. The context of the report was a spectacular rise in crime and poverty in American cities, as well as a shortage in affordable housing, as political will to invest in public housing had waned. The discursive frames and policy recommendations in this report laid much of the groundwork for HOPE VI, urban redevelopment, and neoliberal development that characterized the 1990s and early 2000s. Congressional lawmakers looking for solutions and support from the private sector for the housing crisis were the report's primary audience.
- *HOPE VI: Building Communities and Transforming Lives*—a 1999 promotional report written and distributed by HUD in the later years of the Clinton Administration. At that time, Congress had codified HOPE VI into law for the first time with the Quality Housing and Work Responsibility Act of 1998 (Public Housing Reform Act), marking a move away from the contingent, legally ambiguous appropriations bills that had previously constituted the HOPE VI program. As a result, the Clinton Administration and then-HUD Secretary Andrew Cuomo embarked on a promotional tour to tout the successes and benefits of the program to residents and potential development partners. This report, replete with optimistic visuals and a foreword from Cuomo, was part of that campaign and exemplifies the typical legitimation discourses associated with HOPE VI.

In analyzing the two reports for ideological and discursive elements of participation, neoliberal governance, and racialization, I identify four key rhetorical strategies that legitimate institutional intervention at the expense of participants (table 2.1). The strategies exemplify how the undercurrent of desirability in diversity rhetoric and policy relies concomitantly on policies and rhetorical expressions of undesirability, thereby entrenching hierarchy and difference in favor of institutional managerialism. The strategies

Table 2.1 Legitimation Strategies of Participatory Capture

Legitimation Strategy	*Definition/Function*	*Rhetorical Characteristics*
Participation-as-Cultural Narrative	• Frames participants as to be included in hegemonic cultural narratives • Draws contrasts between desirable populations and populations that threaten hegemonic values	• Appeals to group, national, or cultural "ideals" • Identification with normative values, like family, safety, and consumption • Teleological narratives—using outcomes or purpose to justify action • Modal verbs such as "should," "will," or "must"
Participation-as-Bio/Necropolitics	• Constructs participants in relation to a larger collective body • Emphasizes the biological, physical, and mental capacity of participants • Constructs participants as embodying risk and signifying death—both bodily individual death as well as national or international decay • Casts participants as embodying a social death, threatening the realization of hegemonic values	• Invocation of life-based processes (e.g., life, death, birth, decay, and transformation) • Phrases like "healthy," "revitalization," and "renewal" • Threat construction of the "dangerous" or "endangered" outsider • Affective, descriptive references to (excessive or aberrant) violence, disease, or social/sexual deviance
Participation-as-Diversity Marketing	• Emphasizes enlightenment and progress • Invokes diverse or integrative approaches • signifies "development" or that which *is* developed • Portrays institutional participatory approaches as new and innovative, especially with institutional diversity rather than ethnic diversity in mind	• Metaphoric scientism, marked by phrases like "frontier," "laboratory," and "sophistication" • Futurist discourse (e.g., "new," "modernization," and "creation") • Repetition of the word "diversity" and both its etymological and cultural variants (e.g., "diverse" and "opportunity")
Participation-as-Theodicy	• Signifies an institutional burden or responsibility • Reflects institutional necessity to police values, resources, and populations • Amounts to a defense of the institution's goodness and omnipotence in view of the existence of whatever harm or threat would legitimate intervention	• Genetic fallacy (all good and bad result from the actions or inactions of an institution) • The institution as a frequent subject of a sentence and performing a functional and positive act • (Rhetorical/linguistic) displacement of institutional power when the institution is not the sentence's subject

are: participation-as-cultural narrative, participation-as-bio/necropolitics, participation-as-diversity marketing, and participation-as-theodicy. I view these strategies as heuristic and instructive, inasmuch as they illuminate communicative practices to avoid. After all, as Simmons contends, "rhetoricians and technical communicators involved in policy . . . can use . . . participatory heuristics to help them identify oppressive power relations and look for spaces to intervene" (2007, 134). In the next section, I demonstrate how each legitimation strategy manifested in the rhetoric of HOPE VI federal reports.

HOPE VI'S RHETORICAL LEGITIMATION

Participation-as-Cultural Narrative

Homeownership constituted HOPE VI's predominant cultural narrative. Proponents and policymakers argued the goal of housing in the United States was for a greater number of people to own homes as a way of fulfilling the American Dream and achieving socioeconomic agency. The National Housing Task Force asserted that "Homeownership is a fundamental American ideal" (HUD 1988, 45). HUD stipulated that "Homeownership is vital to long-term neighborhood stability and thus is an important element of most HOPE VI revitalization plans" (HUD 1999, 8). A significant HOPE VI mandate was to present "opportunities for homeownership" (HUD 1999, 3). From a policy perspective in the late 1980s and early 1990s, this position proliferated amid the backdrop of an increase in homelessness, with the corresponding Task Force figuring that "A decent home is the important beginning point for growth into the mainstream of American life" (HUD 1988, 3). In HOPE VI, participation was largely defined by homeownership, which represented one's desirable inclusion into mainstream socioeconomic norms.

In the legitimation strategy, participation-as-cultural narrative, participants are framed as being inducted into hegemonic cultural narratives by way of institutional intervention. In some cases (HOPE VI included), participatory discourse has a constitutive rhetorical effect whereby participants are often pathologized, stereotyped, or cast as emblematic of a larger cultural problem. For HOPE VI, the premise was that poor residents were incapable of self-determination as signified by homeownership. In the neoliberal American context, the discourse of "self-help" crafted a narrative with certain kinds of characters who required institutional management, and as such, "Instead of engaging an already defined and unitary poor subject, each 'self-help' approach proscribes a certain kind of citizen" (Kohl-Arenas 2011, 814). In other words, HOPE VI's process of selective inclusion entailed prescribing particular types of citizens (homeowners, in this case) as being fully and appropriately "American." Moreover, as Kohl-Arenas (2011) contends, "During the neoliberal turn of the 1980s 'self-help' took yet another form as conservative politicians and public intellectuals put forth the now well-worn argument that a bloated welfare state . . . has created deep dependency among the poor" (2011, 814). Thus, in HOPE VI, low-income participants were framed as dependent and lacking in self-help. HUD enacted this framing by appealing to "national" ideals that leveraged hegemonic identification with normative values, like family, safety, and consumption. Moreover, this rhetoric suggests that participatory cultural narratives legitimate institutionalist aims by drawing contrasts between good and bad "kinds," between desirable populations and undesirable populations that threaten hegemonic values. Such threats, in turn, legitimate institutional action.

A Decent Place to Live claimed that "programs to facilitate homeownership and to assist owners in maintaining their properties are key elements in a comprehensive, locally developed housing strategy" (HUD 1988, 47). Years later, HUD adopted this framework and argued that increased access to homeownership would bring the disempowered into the fold of the American economy:

> the flight of . . . families from declining cities weakened local economies, crippled local institutions, and frayed the ties that bind the poor families that remain to the values and the opportunities of mainstream society. In cities across America, HOPE VI is giving these families new reasons to return. (HUD 1999, 8)

These statements allude to white flight from urban areas and imply that, once inner cities were to undergo institutional intervention, they would again be desirable and "normal." Such deployment of selective inclusion invokes a persistent racialized contrast that often "redirects blame for substandard schools, low wages, and scarcity of jobs away from the structural forces that caused these problems while simultaneously reinforcing stereotypes about African American families" (Greenbaum 2019, 2). HUD underscored that "HOPE VI communities are able to compete because they can offer the attributes that most households seek—quality housing, safe streets, good schools, and proximity to shopping and employment" (HUD 1999, 8). Notably, "these families" and "attributes" signify "normally functioning" (i.e., normally participating families)—once more invoking the constitutive nature of participatory rhetorics. HUD drew distinctions between desirable behavior as displayed in some and undesirable behavior as displayed by others. A participant's desirability was determined by their relationship to hegemonic narratives, which had the concurrent effect of naturalizing institutionality while at the same time pathologizing participants.

Participation-as-Bio/Necropolitics

Like the participation-as-cultural narrative whereby participants undergo symbolic and behavioral (mis)alignments with the hegemon, participatory discourses construct participants as parts of a larger collective body. The rhetoric that invokes a collective body emphasizes the biological, physical, and mental capacities of participants. In economic development, participants are often constructed as embodying risk and signifying death—both bodily individual death as well as national or international decay. In this way, participatory discourses are biopolitical. Generally, biopolitics refers to the state's ability to defend society and to regulate human life. Foucault ([1978] 2007) argued that biopolitics was a "management of state forces" that relied upon configuring "populations" whose subjections were defined by "particular biological and pathological features" (367). In the context of federal housing, biopolitics reflects racialized, classed, and gendered methods for determining what "kinds" of people live where and why. At the same time, while the state regulates life, it regulates death also; the state is necropolitical, in that it exercises "the power and the capacity to dictate who may live and who must die" (Mbembe & Meintjes 2003, 161). Participatory discourses are bio/necropolitical when they legitimate interventionist policies, usually by naming a harm to the collective, societal body—be that harm physical or cultural—which is almost always refracted through a "national" or institutional ideal that gives cover to racialized population management (Goldberg 2008; Smith & Vasudevan 2017).

Participants in this legitimation strategy are figured as at-risk by virtue of their exclusion or difference from the hegemonic norm. Conversely, the hegemonic norm is threatened by the "dangerous" or "endangered" outsider. The legitimation of this threat-exclusionary paradigm stems from the bio/necropolitical capacities of the state and its capillary institutions. In HOPE VI, crime and socio-environmental collapse were the threats that the state mandated participation to remedy. In 1988, the Task Force staked their programmatic efficacy on "the vital role that housing plays in human and community development" (HUD 1988, 4). Later, HUD emphasized "the importance of transforming the lives of public housing residents as well as their physical environment" (HUD 1999, 4). Accordingly, participation was very much propagated as essential to achieving full-fledged agency and humanity for the excluded, as HOPE VI promoted "human development" contingent upon "place" in society, which could be transformed as one's "life" also could be transformed.

Crime was the impediment (i.e., the threat) that participatory mixed-income housing would overcome. *A Decent Place to Live* painted a bleak picture of the excluded zones of America's underdeveloped. Referencing drug-related crime in urban America, the Task Force wrote, "The plague of drug use and drug dealing must be confronted" (HUD 1988, 3). They refer to gang-related activity as "domestic terrorism" and weave an existential crisis in which

> some urban neighborhoods, housing projects—both public and private—have been reduced to contested turf, dominated by battles between gangs, between drug pushers, between any two people with a gripe and weapons. Children walk to school in fear of being shot; they are recruited to serve as drug dealers and prostitutes. (HUD 1988, 10)

With a gesture toward the policy imperative of the state, the Task Force recommended "the range of anti-drug, law enforcement and related actions . . . be taken to stop the violence" (HUD 1988, 11). They go on to say, "Just as a national task force to combat terrorism was convened in 1985 . . . a similar high-level effort against domestic terrorism is needed today" (HUD 1988, 11). To deal with these threats to the nation, and "In order to ensure success, local government must participate in identifying and carrying out solutions" (HUD 1988, 34). Lastly, the Task Force's participatory discourse reflects a paradoxical structure of exclusion/inclusion, when they write

> that the persistence of intolerable conditions in even a very few projects blights not only the lives of the people who live in them and the neighborhoods in which they fester, but the entire effort to house low-income people in the United States. (HUD 1988, 34)

Such framing of participants as risks-at-risk reveals that, as participatory discourses take root (especially in healthcare and housing, for instance), participation can be framed to hinge on the axis of life and death.

The intervention that the federal government made in these matters was framed as one of necessity since, according to HUD, "without access to the jobs, the support services, or the transportation that would enable residents to move up and out—we should not have been surprised when these projects failed" (HUD 1999, 3). HUD was "committed to ensuring that residents at all HOPE VI sites have access to the information, expertise, and support they need to participate fully at every step of the redevelopment process" and "rather than reinvest in failure, build new communities. Start from the ground up" (HUD 1999, 3). In this participatory framework, the intervention provides the tools for the underdeveloped to participate, and this participation solves both deficit and threat. The excluded are transformed by virtue of participatory interventionism, since with HOPE VI, participants have "the power to see a better future" (HUD 1999, 11). In other parts of the federal reports, residents are framed as "poverty-stricken" dependents who can "transform" and be "strong," "as first-time homeowners . . . no longer weighed down by isolation and despair [and] able to realize the American Dream for themselves and their families" (HUD 1999, 11). HUD thus accentuates its role in mediating life and death by contrasting pre-intervention, underdeveloped residents against full-fledged, healthily functioning Americans.

Equally important, individual transformations mirrored a neoliberal transformation of the state and its institutions. Specifically, the transformation totaled a move toward self-sufficiency and a sort of de-public-ing that matched that of the housing market, as engineered by the federal government. According to HUD, HOPE VI services "show prospective homebuyers how to clean up their credit and maintain their home, equipping them with the knowledge they will need to become astute homeseekers, qualified mortgage applicants, and successful owners" (HUD 1999, 11). In moments like these, *A Decent Place to Live* evoked a series of metamorphoses wherein residents will develop and evolve from mere residents to full participants in the housing market. Public housing serves as a cocoon for a homebuying butterfly. Elsewhere, HUD employed the metaphor of a sociopolitical ladder, along which residents were expected to ascend at last from state-dependent to independent citizen: "HOPE VI provides a ladder of assistance to residents of distressed public housing, for whom the climb out of dependence to self-sufficiency can be particularly tricky" (HUD 1999, 12).

HUD also highlighted how HOPE VI sites supposedly helped "entrepreneurial public housing residents become small business owners" (HUD 1999, 13). This emphasis on entrepreneurialism ultimately instituted a second layer of exclusion because it added an individual deficit on top of a cultural one. For example, HUD wrote,

> HOPE VI developments are being enriched with a vast array of resources and services that can help any motivated resident climb toward a better future—but motivation is the key. Many housing authorities have established rigorous admission requirements for HOPE VI communities. (HUD 1999, 14)

These requirements meant that

> the housing authority may require that public housing residents be in a self-sufficiency program that sets clear goals for moving toward independence. Like any private landlord, most housing authorities demand that residents do not have a recent history of abusing their lease, their credit, or the law. (HUD 1999, 14)

In this case, participation functioned as both a means and an end. The excluded are made agential by participating in institutional processes so that, in the end, the excluded may participate as a state of being and thereby maintain their own lives as well as the life of the institution.

Participation-as-Diversity Marketing

Diversity marketing is generally understood as marketing to diverse audiences, which requires "acknowledging that marketing and advertising must offer alternative ways of communicating to diverse groups" ("Diversity Marketing" 2020). Participatory discourses frequently extend past marginalized groups of people and refer additionally to entire organizations or sub-institutions. According to Kohl-Arenas,

> While participatory processes of the 1960s were often aimed (at least in language) at confronting and gaining access to unequal power structures, modern day participatory processes are designed primarily to build trust, relationships, or to "integrate" once "isolated" populations into the global marketplace. (2011, 815)

Mohan and Stokke (2000) make similar conceptual links between neoliberal institutional participation and decentralization. Neoliberal participation means involving a greater number of organizations (typically, private institutions) with the added aim of diffusing accountability. When "organisational arrangements for decentralisation include, in order, privatisation, deregulation, delegation, devolution, and deconcentration," they argue, "the notion of participation in state decision making . . . means market transactions" (2000, 248). Put another way, participation represents an impulse to totalize power "based on a harmony model of power" (Mohan & Stokke 2000, 249).

Beyond organizational harmony, however, a key aspect of diversity marketing is an emphasis on enlightenment and progress, such that the communicator, in calling upon diverse or integrative approaches, signifies "development" or that which is developed from a techno-intellectual standpoint. Coupled with consistent appeals to racial and ethnic diversity, participatory aspects of HOPE VI relied heavily on the portrayal of its participatory approaches as "new" and "innovative," especially with institutional diversity rather than simply ethnic diversity in mind. To be clear, rhetorical uses of futurity and innovation retain a racialized character, given the fraught legacy of terms like "primitive" and "backward" to refer to colonized and enslaved peoples. Thus, while marketing claims of exigent and exciting products are nothing new, in the case of HOPE VI, it does demonstrate a discursive relationship between the developed (i.e., the enlightened, the innovative, the progressed) and all the socioeconomic machinations of mixed-income housing, namely neoliberal decentralization. As a result of this relationship, the HOPE VI participatory scheme suggests that an interventionist legitimation as applied to instances of socioeconomic "failure" or deficit allows the state and institutions to undergo their own transformations. This allowance potentially curtails democratic and legal avenues for implementing state accountability, because the state can promote undemocratic outcomes while proclaiming participation-based progress, as it did in HOPE VI when HUD espoused belief in "the capacity to foster communities with a diversity that fulfills the promise of America" (HUD 1999, 8). This diversity was just as reflected in diversity of organizational and institutional input as it was reflected in ethnic numbers games. In rhetorical terms, participation-as-diversity marketing manifests as metaphoric scientism (marked by phrases like "frontier," "laboratory," and "sophistication") and as futurist discourse (e.g., "new," "modernization," and "creation").

It is therefore particularly significant that HOPE VI's organizational diversity was marketed as a new frontier in institutional configuration. "In addition to its tremendous significance as an urban revitalization tool," HUD argued, "HOPE VI is the laboratory in which the future of public housing is being tested today" (HUD 1999, 16). The mixed-income approach was touted as the cutting edge of planning and urban problem-solving. This cutting-edge aspect relied on participation for legitimation, since, "A primary explanation for the mixed-income and, increasingly, mixed-use nature of HOPE VI revitalization plans is the growing sophistication among grantees and their financial advisors in obtaining and coordinating diverse public and private funding sources" (HUD 1999, 16). Furthermore, HUD stated, "One of the lasting legacies of HOPE VI will be that grantees, residents, partners, and other stakeholders are working together to creatively transform America's worst public housing into 'communities of opportunity' for the new millennium" (HUD 1999, 16). Participation for HOPE VI and HUD was most valued when it instantiated an institutional imperative to fashion itself anew amid intensified coordination of various organizational actors.

This techno-intellectual imperative had been established at least since the Task Force's 1988 report, which also argued for participatory mixed-income programs on grounds of innovative institutionality. The Task Force referred to a decentralized, localized formula as a "new era of cooperation" (HUD 1988, 12). Promoting mixed-income developments as a "modernization program," the Task Force wrote,

> The combination of effort by these public and private entities constitutes a 'new wave' of initiative and resourcefulness in meeting our critical housing needs. Vigorous and diverse, it raises new possibilities and new hope for housing low- and moderate-income families. (HUD 1988, 33, 10)

In heralding the state's domain of enlightenment and epistemic authority, *A Decent Place to Live* called for a "new spirit of cooperation" that "should arise between the federal government and private owners of assisted housing in order to preserve . . . housing for low-income residents" (HUD 1988, 12).

In gesturing toward organizational participation, the Task Force remarked, "Local financial institutions, the business community and religious organizations are all important players in this 'new wave' of local initiatives" (HUD 1988, 19). This innovation referred heavily to the democratization of finance and securities instruments. "The new wave is characterized by new sources of money," the Task Force wrote, "new ways to cut construction costs and new techniques to reduce barriers to affordable housing" (HUD 1988, 19). In terms of the federal government's role in housing finance, the Task Force labeled it a "new delivery system" and noted that "the rise of this new system could not have happened without substantial federal assistance" (HUD 1988, 19). HOPE VI's participatory discourse indicates a dual function of diversity marketing—a function that communicates diversity as participation in identity-based liberalism and also one that relies on appeals to "innovation" and the "new" to signal the enlightenment and competence of the institution.

Participation-as-Theodicy

In a general sense, participatory discourses imply an institutional burden or responsibility to problem-solve by recruiting others to participate. In some cases, this burden is managerial (e.g., participatory design in workplace settings). In others, this burden can be more values-based (e.g., a community organizer who engages in participatory action research). Such burdens reflect the hegemonic and presumptive imposition of statist logics whereby values and materiality are institutionally mediated. Indeed, participatory practitioners often make decisions on behalf of institutions. The institutional necessity, then, to police values, resources, and populations represents a theodicean quality. If theodicy is the "defense of God's goodness and omnipotence in view of the existence of evil," as *Merriam-Webster* would have it, then participation here amounts to a defense of the institution's goodness and omnipotence in view of the existence of whatever harm or threat legitimates intervention or concern.

In the case of HOPE VI, the theodicean quality manifests as a duty on the part of the federal government to create favorable conditions that would support a homeownership society. Crucially, though, this federal duty is construed as supporting private finance and decentralization such that, ultimately, the federal government's role is mitigated or obscured even as the role remains central. This arrangement—both materially and discursively—indicates that an underlying neoliberal approach pervades institutional complexity, especially when it comes to mixed-income housing. The federal move toward financial securitization and democratization was certainly central to mixed-income housing, and the National Housing Task Force believed that "The simple device of pledging the full faith and credit of the federal government revolutionized the nation's housing system by making possible long-term mortgages at a fixed cost with low down payments—turning America into a nation of homeowners" (HUD 1988, 9). The Task Force doubled down on federal intervention when they wrote, "What is missing is adequate participation by the federal partner" and "Today, we need a renewed federal commitment to capitalize on the private sector's growing body of experience in producing and rehabilitating low-income housing through its partnership with the public sector" (HUD 1988, 9–10). They even offered that "the federal government is the pivotal force in meeting housing needs and must be the principal source of funding" (HUD 1988, 11). At the same time, however, for the Task Force, the federal government would be essential only insofar as it facilitated wider participatory institutionalism.

The discursive interplay between facilitation and necessity on the part of the federal government signified a defense of the institution's omnipotence and its capacity both to transcend and permeate the larger system. According to the Task Force, "This [federal] capacity can be used to develop new alliances among the public, private and community sectors to produce and preserve affordable housing" (HUD 1988, 10). In this regard, the alliance would consist of "civic and religious groups and national and local nonprofit organizations that would help facilitate the delivery of housing opportunity to those who need it" (HUD 1988, 10). The Task Force additionally advocated a housing system based "on the understanding that government closest to the people is best situated to identify and respond to needs and conditions—especially the conditions of local housing markets" (HUD 1988, 11). This participatory approach was endemic to HOPE VI over the program's lifespan. In 1999, HUD described HOPE VI as

> collaborative, enlisting a wide range of stakeholders—including mayors and other elected officials, resident organizations, developers and lenders, government agencies, nonprofit and faith-based groups, and many others—in partnerships that marry public goals, private-sector energy and funding, and the dormant hopes of community residents. (HUD 1999, 5)

This deferential role prescribed by the federal government ironically figures the federal government as the primary determinant of participation while it also advocates for its own reduced role (i.e., decentralized approaches to centralized outcomes). From an institutional standpoint, this ironic aspect further complicates the distinction between participant/non-participant and further emphasizes the primacy of institutional power in dictating who participates as well as how and why.

Finally, the connection between participation and finance cannot be overstated. In the documents analyzed in this chapter, the federal government's primary role is seen as setting the stage for a broader approach to housing finance that relied on the federal government to arrange a market. Reflecting diversity marketing, the Task Force stated, "The principle of using federal funds to leverage other investment is key to the new partnership and a new element in federal housing policy" (HUD 1988, 11). The members of the Task Force recommended "direct expenditures in the forms of loans and grants to reduce the capital cost of housing; rental assistance . . . tax incentives . . . federal insurance and guarantees" (HUD 1988, 11). Moreover, they asserted, "The federal government has been an essential partner—sometimes a silent partner—by providing low-income tax credits, tax-exempt financing, rental assistance and below market-rate loans that make projects feasible and affordable to the poor" (HUD 1988, 19). Similarly, the Task Force advocated that "To encourage maximum participation by all sectors of the housing delivery system, including private and nonprofit developers, public housing authorities should be permitted to use up to 25 percent of [federally provided] funds" (HUD 1988, 20). In other words, the legitimation used in HOPE VI relied on an institutional omnipotence that manifested in both the program's rhetoric as well as the program's material outcomes.

The sprawl of financialization matched the sprawl of institutional involvement. This involvement was seemingly based on the imperative of one institution: the federal government. Underscoring the federal government's omnipotent role in assuming the risk burden of America's expanding mortgage and finance systems, *A Decent Place to Live* reads, "The federal housing finance system has evolved into an efficient mechanism for linking the mortgage market with domestic and international capital markets" (HUD 1988, 52). Despite the assumption of federal risk and the proliferation of federal funds, however, the Task Force recommended a "minimum of regulation and maximum of flexibility to meet distinctive local housing needs" (HUD 1988, 19). In the state's such mystified institutional reach lies the theodicean aspect of HOPE VI's participation: the coordination of financial instruments and funding across a multitude of organizations, with the backing of the federal government. For participatory rhetorics and participatory capture, more broadly, theodicean qualities potentially obscure the determinative roles that participating organizations play in facilitating the harms those same organizations seek to solve. On one hand, participatory rhetorics can obscure the central, God-like powers (material, institutional, or discursive) at work in certain programs and initiatives. On the other hand, participatory rhetorics can leverage that tendency to obscure either by diffusing accountability throughout wider systems or by ascribing primary agency to one entity. The potential harm is that those most vulnerable or subject to institutional imperative are denied both recognition and recompense.

CONCLUSION

HUD still relies on participation as a managerial tool for navigating racialization and marginalization. In January 2023, for instance, HUD proposed a new rule for "strengthening the participation of Tribes and Tribal organizations in HUD's housing counseling program" (HUD 2023, para. 2). The rule essentially expands eligibility for those wanting to be federal housing counselors to include greater Native representation in housing counseling programs for Native Americans. HUD framed the proposed rule itself as an increase in participation, but the Department also pointed to participatory methods like "consultation and listening sessions" with Native organizations as especially productive in bringing about the proposal. Skepticism, however, abounded during at least one of the listening sessions. An audience member questioned HUD's methodology, arguing that "HUD's generic utilization of a counseling program contrived 28 years before tribes had the tools to develop our own programs is wrought with issues" (HUD 2021, 9). The audience member continued that "even though fair housing laws do not apply in tribal communities, the burdensome requirements placed on tribes to comply with outdated legislation in effect creates and further perpetuates a notably unfair housing climate for reservation-based communities" (HUD 2021, 9). The exchange highlights persistent tension in institutional and organizational deployments of participation: participatory rhetoric and methods have reinscribed the hierarchical difference it seeks to confront. To be sure, information derived from participatory methods can be useful for practitioners and researchers. For marginalized people, however, such labor is at once both a step removed from and an acute reminder of the realities of exclusion.

In the previous chapter, I asked, "How do organizations mobilize conceptions of diversity and participation to navigate racial and cultural difference in public engagement?" In seeking an answer, I analyzed the rhetoric of a participatory federal housing program for discourses related to participatory capture, neoliberal governance, and racialization. Four legitimation strategies were identified. First, participatory discourses often rely on cultural narratives that validate mainstream or larger values. In the case of HOPE VI, its cultural narrative was homeownership in relation to values like the American Dream and socioeconomic agency. Second, participatory discourses retain a bio/necropolitical character, as the exigence for participatory approaches is usually to address some threat—physical, cultural, or otherwise that the state or institution must address with an interventionist stance. For HOPE VI, the threats invoked are crime, drugs, violence, and low moral capacity, which, in context, invariably carry racialized meanings. Attaching economic and cultural deficit to certain populations legitimates interventionism that figures said populations as wards of institutional imperative. Moreover, such discourse naturalizes racial and segregationist consequences, since,

> While recognizing that media-produced terms such as "gang banger" and "welfare queen" refer to the racial/gendered subalterns, they read them as codes for racial difference that mask the racially exclusionary aims of the legislation and policy initiatives these terms are deployed to support. (Silva 2007, 264)

Third, participatory discourses function as diversity marketing—not just racially or ethnically, but also organizationally. In the HOPE VI literature, in fact, diversity is an institutionalist concern rather than a communitarian one. Lastly, participatory discourses carry a theodicean quality, in that participatory institutionalism can obscure or absolve institutions of their uniquely determinative roles in complex systems.

Despite its implications of democracy and service, participation has historically been imbued with issues of power that should prompt researchers to continue interrogating the origins, motivations, and effects of one of the field's most prominently discussed methodologies in relation to social justice. Haas and Eble (2018) defined the social justice turn in technical and professional communication as a "turn toward a collective disciplinary redressing of social injustice sponsored by rhetorics and practices that infringe upon, neglect, withhold, and/or abolish human, non-human animal, and environmental rights" (2018, 5). Additionally, they argue social justice practitioners should pursue "more critical understandings of . . . systems of and rhetorics of hegemonic power—and how and why they have historically shaped how we regard specific cultures and communities in relation to their technical and scientific expertise or lack thereof" (2018, 12). In another contribution to the social justice turn, Moore (2018) advocates for "participatory design, participatory action research, and the many approaches to teaching students to ethically engage with communities . . . [in contrast to] top-down decision-making and design structures" (2018, 193). Rose and Cardinal (2021) maintain that "Choosing a more participatory approach shifts the perspective that people are research subjects or sources of information to one where they are collaborators and co-designers" because doing so, in their view, "allows the people who are engaged in the research endeavor to have more agency and say in the process" (85). But what does it say about a methodology that purports a social justice aim on one hand but on the other relies on processes of institutional mediation to negotiate the limits of agency?

Given that participation assumes immutable difference, is participation just diversity management, and if so, in what ways does participation re-entrench notions of undesirability as applied to racialized or economically otherized subjects? To what degree has participation become so institutionalized that its methods and rhetorics allow neoliberal governmentality to continue, as one critic observed, "incorporating its own critiques. . . . absorbing and partially neutralising disruptive difference, turned into governable, benign difference?" (Bilge 2020, 326). The legitimation strategies discussed in this chapter reinforce that technical communication has a far from benign role in potentially perpetuating benign difference.

The imperative for designers and communicators to turn a critical lens upon ourselves is salient amid the neoliberal trend to institutionalize social justice. Participation, as a broader organizational approach, evokes the entrenched frameworks of diversity and inclusion, which critical scholars have identified as often working against the people they purport to help. Nash (2019), for instance, claims that the university's incorporation of difference is a "key rhetoric animating an institution's self-presentation and organization [while signifying] an institution's own commitment to inclusion. . . . as evidence of an institution's transformation" (2019, 23). Similarly, Ahmed (2012) argues that

> to work for institutions, as practitioners do, can require that you develop a habit of talking mission talk, what we can call "happy talk," a way of telling a happy story of the institution that is at once a story of the institution as happy. (2012, 10)

What's lost in happy talk is often the symbolic and material violences carried out in the institution's perpetuation. In Ahmed's study of diversity, for example, she assesses that diversity facilitates the institutionalization of Whiteness, with recruitment functioning "as a technology for the reproduction of whiteness" (2012, 39). Participation can function in much the same way, since, after all, participants are recruited. Thus, I ask further, how might participation function as a technology for the reproduction of marginalization? Is participation a method for change, or is it bound to institutionalism—hyperpragmatist in its unique ability to avoid being critically understood as such?

Chapter 3

"Broader Horizons"

Deficit and Governance Models in HOPE VI Community Building

Ultimately, the U.S. federal government codified its programmatic approach to community building in two key documents: *Community Building in Public Housing: Ties that Bind People and Their Communities* (1997) and *HOPE VI: Community Building Makes a Difference* (2000). *Community Building in Public Housing* is a 100-page handbook primarily attributed to development and social work scholar Arthur Naparstek (1938–2004), formerly a frequent consultant to federal and congressional housing advocates. Other document preparers listed are the social policy think tank Urban Institute as well as the now-defunct Aspen Systems Corporation, an information management firm purchased by technology and defense contractor Lockheed Martin in 2005. The book contains a foreword by then-U.S. Secretary of Housing and Urban Development Andrew Cuomo, in which he writes, "Community building . . . involves residents in setting goals and shaping strategies to achieve them. Community building starts not with deficit or problem-oriented thinking, but with identifying the unique set of assets that a particular area possesses" (HUD 1997, iii). Cuomo identifies the audience for the handbook as "public housing managers and all individuals and organizations concerned with the physical and social revitalization of American communities" (HUD 1997, iii). The book begins with an introduction to the general concept of community building and then outlines processes for implementing a community-building paradigm at local levels. Those processes are: Preparing a Mission Statement, Naming a Community-Building Facilitator, Creating a Representative Community Organization, Assuring that Management is Connected and Responsive to Residents, and Modifying the Physical Setting. Importantly, the publication frames resident participation as an institutional management process wherein residents participate via governance or through recognized local organizational bodies like associations and councils.

Community Building Makes a Difference is a similar document, a ninety-six-page status report also attributed to Arthur Naparstek. An introduction by then-U.S. Senator Barbara Mikulski identifies the audience as "not only public housing staff and residents, but also . . . local and national policymakers, along with private-sector community stakeholders, community-based nonprofit organizations, advocacy groups . . . [and] service providers" (HUD 2000, vi). As a report, *Community Building Makes a Difference* is more evaluative than instructional, and its goal is to illustrate the successes and "lessons learned" from HUD's community-building approach. A secondary purpose of the report is to show that community building achieves its objectives. In his foreword to this report, Cuomo contextualizes community building as "an approach that combats the isolation of public housing residents" by promoting "mainstream opportunities," "self-sufficiency," and "partnerships among housing authorities, residents, local organizations, and the business community" (HUD 2000, i). Accordingly, the document contains many visual and narrative examples of joyful residents, many of whom are Black women who, for instance, "learn childcare skills," move from "welfare to work," and display "entrepreneurial crafts."

In the following sections, I reflect on these discursive and organizational elements of HOPE VI's participatory capture. My analysis found that, in their manuals, HUD employed two models of participation (deficit and governance) (table 3.1) by appealing to values of self-sufficiency, which implied that local communities undergoing redevelopment were underdeveloped and were lacking in capability. Deficit models paradoxically and disingenuously place responsibility on local communities, while also using discursive strategies of exceptionalism and benevolence. Governance models build on these strategies and limit participation to forms of tokenism and representation. Importantly, given that HOPE VI's calls for participation presupposed the inferiority of its disproportionately impacted Black women participants, the racialized animation of HOPE VI's participatory discourse cannot be ignored in understanding how participatory capture relies on structures of hierarchy.

With racialized hierarchy in mind, calls to participate promulgate the "fetish of transparency," or the idea that each individual is capable of achieving a standard ontological position centered upon agency (Northover 2012, 68). The concept of agency itself, however, is bound up with non-agency; and, appeals to a universal (or transparent) agency legitimate hierarchical social structures, setting the stage for institutional, racialized exploitation. Definitions and exercises of agency often rely on renderings of what agency is not. In applications of power within socially stratified contexts, one kind of (empowered) subject is figured as a fully functional social "ideal" while at the same time a non-subject (in need of empowerment) is figured as a dysfunctional social "aberration." Regarding racial formation in the United

Table 3.1 Deficit and Governance Models of Community Engagement in HOPE VI Manuals

Model #1: Development-from-Deficit

Example Methods

- Tasking of residents (enlisting residents as laborers or performers)
- Ethnographic cataloging
- Community service projects

Rhetorical and Discursive Characteristics

- Appeals to individualist exceptionalism
- Ideographs such as "self-sufficiency" or "entrepreneurialism"
- Depicts institutions as saviors
- Aligns the interest of residents with the interests of more powerful stakeholders
- Figures participants as "resources" or "assets"
- Stipulates participant independence as contingent on institutional benevolence or the bestowal of agency onto participants
- Ascribes immutable cultural characteristics onto participants
- Negates or displaces social networks implemented prior to intervention

Model #2: Governance/Deliberation

Example Methods

- Resident councils
- Representative organizations
- Meetings
- Trainings
- Surveys

Rhetorical and Discursive Characteristics

- Emphasizes "collaborations" and "partnerships" among organizations
- Assumes utilitarian ethos in problem-solving
- Appropriates functionalist phrasing like "benchmarking," "order," "purpose," "goals," and "objectives"
- Constitutes residents as exceptions that mandate institutional action
- Recruits (identifies) participants in the maintenance/sovereignty of institutions

States, Hartman (1997) contends that the criminalization and stigmatization of Black agency allows the state to "obfuscate[e] its instrumental role in terror by projecting all culpability and wrongdoing onto the [formally] enslaved" (1997, 82). Linkages between raciality and power, between participation and influence reflect how, for racialized institutions like U.S. federal housing,

> states of violence and poverty would be explained by the irrationality of the resisters of the life of freedom, by the unreasonableness of the colonized mind, or by the idiosyncratic immoral or irresponsible nature of persons unfortunately stricken by aberrations. (Northover 2012, 75)

Consequently, immorality, irrationality, and lack of social fitness are discursive strategies steeped in raciality, or broadly "signifiers of racial and cultural difference" (Silva 2009, 219). Such signifiers are invoked to justify state violence and population management such as the segregationist housing policies that preceded public housing crises and broader shifts to neoliberal programs like HOPE VI that ultimately relied on tropes and visions of aberrant, Black criminality. Consequently, calls for the subaltern or the aberrant to participate have the potential to lay culpability for violence and poverty not with the state for exclusionary or exploitative policies but with the subaltern for being at a naturalized ontological deficit. Emphasis on the deficit of marginalized groups potentially obscures the role of organizational, institutional, and policy actions that create and sustain inequality.

In the case of HOPE VI, the state's claim of provisioning tools "of empowerment," for instance, presupposes a universality, an abstract equality, that positions the racial Other as naturally lacking, "that the targets of the development project [e.g., poverty, crime] resulted from certain peoples' and places' *natural* incapacity to move forward on their own" (Silva 2015, 36). This rhetoric of development, reflective of idealized notions of agency and self-determination, "writes the 'others of Europe's' failure to achieve human beings' highest vocation because of how the laws of nature prevent them from even contemplating the highest principles and values according to universal reason" (Silva 2015, 35); in other words, the rhetoric of development in this regard states to the subaltern: *since you are incapable of achieving on your own, the state or institution will do it for you, to you, or on your behalf.* Participation is one such statement expressed at the levels of discourse and organizational methodology in HOPE VI. In the following sections, I present my analysis of the HOPE VI manuals. First, I articulate the discursive elements of the deficit model of development. I show how HOPE VI appealed to themes of self-sufficiency and "assets" to justify its institutional intervention. Next, I describe the governance model of development as it appears in the practices and discourses of HOPE VI. The governance model reformulated top-down hierarchical methods as "participatory" by emphasizing representative forms of deliberation like resident councils that relied on appeals to exceptionalism. Both models are instances of participatory capture that demonstrate how power, raciality, and organizational communication influence contested policy outcomes.

SELF-SUFFICIENCY, CULTURAL DEFICIT, AND ASSETS

HUD's discourse minimized the contentiousness of its relationship to public housing residents. The department's goal was to displace undesirable residents and to privilege the ones that conformed to HOPE VI's institutional mandates. This dynamic inherently pits residents against developers. This oppositional relationship, though, stems from persistent anti-poor, antiblack public policies. As a result,

> the attitudes of the poor toward municipal authorities are . . . rooted in deeper histories, tied to community power relations linked to class, race, and gender inequities that long predate anything known as HOPE VI but still help to condition its reception. (Vale 2019, 33)

HUD sought to increase its organizational and programmatic control by implementing a development-from-deficit participatory model that signaled participation but configured residents as unworthy of determining their own physical communities.

In legitimating this model, HOPE VI's community-building manuals stressed entrepreneurialism, once more obscuring the larger, deliberate market forces and public policies that were central to the formation of segregated neighborhoods. Not surprisingly, the rhetoric of these documents further suggests that "enhanced and broadened participation can sometimes lead to genuine power sharing, but sometimes may yield little more than an illusion of inclusion, masking the increased domination of private economic actors" (Vale 2019, 42). HOPE VI claimed harsh budgetary environments as the impetus to rely more on the private sector and on residents themselves, whom HOPE VI rhetorically positioned as "resources." *Community Building Makes a Difference* opens with the statement that, "Declining Federal housing subsidies and the advent of welfare reform are bringing dramatic changes to the funding environment for public housing." The document continues, "As traditional sources of revenue diminish, public housing managers are re-examining a previously little-used resource: the energy and efforts of residents of public housing themselves" (HUD 2000, 1). Self-reliance was one of HOPE VI's core political values. For HOPE VI, the goal of self-sufficiency was "to provide residents in [low-income] areas with the opportunity to learn and acquire the skills needed to achieve self-sufficiency." Another related goal was "community sweat equity—to instill in these Americans the belief that with economic self-sufficiency comes an obligation to self-responsibility and giving back to one's community" (HUD 2000, v). On the surface, HUD's discourse strategies implied a reduced role for institutions.

After all, community building was framed as "predicated on the idea that residents must take control of their destiny and the destiny of their communities" (HUD 1997, v). HUD wrote that community building was "built on efforts to help residents take on new responsibilities, make new connections with the larger community, get and retain jobs, start their own profitable businesses, and even own their own homes" (HUD 1997, vi). Additionally, in referencing the budgetary environment, the authors of *Community Building Makes a Difference* wrote that "Today's changing policy environment is causing public housing managers to seek new ways to accomplish the traditional goals of providing decent, low-cost housing and helping residents to move toward independence" (HUD 2000, 7). With these comments, it seems that HUD supported the self-determination of communities and signaled support for economic and cultural independence. However, both comments suggest that community building refers more strongly to individual assimilation into desired institutional contexts rather than to communal independence from institutionalist economic planning. The result of this reference is a subtle rhetorical effect that asserts two messages: the first is that individual success/freedom depends on institutional intervention, such that the individual must act in accordance with institutionalist mandates in order to achieve a level of apparent independence; and, the second is that, because the institutionalist aims are set in opposition to the community (which is configured a priori as deficient), the immutable characteristics of the community are to be blamed for any failures. With this strategy, HOPE VI encouraged a deficit model of development—one that figured residents as blameworthy for their communities' ills.

At the same time, the program's participatory mandate was justified with the argument that the residents could take care of themselves, with the condition, of course, that residents meet the appropriate requirements that not only enabled institutional sanction but also reduced institutional accountability. Along those lines, according to legal scholar Nicolás M. Perrone (2017), "A basic premise of neoliberal governmentality is that investors need to be blind to the social consequences of their actions" (2017, 7). In the state-aided privatization schemes of neoliberalism, accountability is implied and prefigured almost to the point of being nonexistent or imperceptible. Accordingly, low-income residents must be made to be at a deficit, both materially and ontologically, as seen in the discourse of HOPE VI, a regime that operated under a diminished accountability that was central to its function. The purpose of HOPE VI was to make the "hand" of the state as invisible as that of the market; and, to achieve these aims, accountability had to be diffused away from the state and, discursively, onto the mostly Black residents whose purported deficiencies mandated state intervention from the start. From that vantage, the development-from-deficit model persisted in representing institutional action as a savior for an incompetent, deficient population, with HUD arguing that, "Public housing communities can become effective training grounds and launching pads for underprivileged or marginalized citizens who want to become self-sufficient and a catalyst for the revitalization of the larger neighborhood" (HUD 2000, 61).

In gesturing toward participatory capture, critics see the discursive iteration of "community" as particularly debilitating to marginalized groups because such appeals limit the agency of those deemed community members, at the same time that they make certain "kinds" of people visible within an institutional purview. Williams (2004) argues that the reliance on narratives of "community" represents an "uncritical celebration" in participatory development. Moreover, in that respect,

> the danger here is that what are often arbitrary divisions of space are naturalised, and the power effects of these divisions are ignored. Those who don't fit into easily demarcated and territorial "communities" can all too easily fall foul of visions of development, participatory or otherwise. (2004, 561)

Mohan and Stokke concur, saying, "instead of romanticising the role of local civil society in development theory and practice, we need to examine the political use of 'the local' by various actors" (2000, 254). At issue, then, are the ways in which "community" formulates certain locales and groups of people into monolithic states of exception that legitimate institutional actions, even when (and often because) those actions bring about negative material consequences for groups inhabiting certain spaces. Once more, in HOPE VI's worldview,

> "communities" are not merely given naturalised boundaries, they are also idealised in terms of their content. Social norms are seen as part of a "local culture" for development programmes to respond to, without necessarily unpacking that culture, or seeing it as the product of internalised power relationships. (Williams 2004, 562)

This constitutive function of participatory discourse—naming populations and bestowing the stigma of failure upon them—enables institutions to shirk accountability in how they (fail to effectively) collaborate with marginalized groups and places.

In relying on this constitutive function in its discourse, participatory capture naturalizes institutional action by arguing either that certain communities need intervention and/or that their purported social failures result from natural, cultural deficiencies. These discourses impute institutional values onto both the subjects and audiences of such rhetorical appeals. In this regard, despite complexity (i.e., "the overlapping, shifting and subjective nature of 'communities' and the permeability of boundaries"), "The 'community' in participatory approaches to development is often conceptualized as some kind of natural, desirable social entity imbued with all sorts of desirable values and the simple manifestation of this in organizational form" (Cleaver 1999, 603). At the same time, however, "Concepts of 'the individual' underlying participatory approaches swings widely between 'rational choice' and 'social being' models" (Cleaver 1999, 600). Herein, accordingly, lies yet another paradox that marks the nature of exclusion/inclusion within participatory approaches and how they can lead to capture: cultures and communities are often deemed deficient based upon failure to enact individual rationality (i.e., agency). Thus, this lack of agency mandates institutionalist-statist intervention, construed as "participation." Likewise, in participatory development,

> Culture is variously perceived as a constraint . . . the "glue" which keeps the community together . . . and a resource to be tapped in development. . . It has already been seen how institutions are at once supposed to develop from weak "traditional" forms to strong modern forms whilst at the same time remaining culturally embedded. (Cleaver 1999, 604)

In HOPE VI's community building, low-income, Black communities were discursively and programmatically barred from the sovereign rationality and determinism of the state, even as they were enlisted to legitimate the state's methods. Indeed, cultural deficit operated at a fixed position within the organization's institutional, interventionist stratagem; this cultural fixedness is a pillar of participatory capture because it constrains both the voice and influence of the marginalized, especially when those most vulnerable are discursively and materially rendered as inferior or at a deficit.

The aspect that prevails in community building's participatory rhetoric is that the residents altogether lack sovereignty, thus allowing for benevolent intervention on the parts of institutional stakeholders. In other words, the residents' independence was contingent upon a forced, interventionist salvation that rewarded those who conformed to institutional imperatives. The community-building protocols advise facilitators to prioritize participation from better-qualified residents. In this way, the program advocates a strain of individualist exceptionalism that reflects a more affective rendering of a racialized, neoliberal ethos. In a "Resident Involvement" sub-section of one of the manuals, the authors write,

> Residents should be actively involved from the start in identifying the needs and priorities of the community and shaping and implementing the strategies for addressing them. Failure to include residents lengthens the process and quite often leads to lawsuits. The best people must be continually sought out and nurtured to fulfill this critical role. (HUD 2000, 61)

Extending from the belief that the "best" participants were those that reduced programmatic friction and confrontation with powerful stakeholders, the conflation of participation and expediency in HOPE VI's approach suggests a structural misalignment between institutional objectives and communal potential.

Specifically, the language of national "assets" (i.e., the naming and identifying of "assets") served a constitutive function in that it allowed more powerful stakeholders to lay claim to exercising authority over a geographically chartered constituency. HUD argued that,

> Residents of public housing could help stretch Federal dollars by assisting with such necessary programs as childhood disease immunization, tutoring and cleanup, along with tasks that might lead to permanent employment, such as routine repairs . . . or remodeling. (HUD 2000, 21)

HUD justified this "tasking" of residents by gesturing toward an innate productivity that was initially supposed to have been lacking. The Department wrote, "By linking self-sufficiency with responsibility to one's community, HOPE VI opened the door to a previously unacknowledged and tragically underutilized asset of PHAs [public housing authorities] around the Nation" (HUD 2000, 21). Moreover, based upon HUD's deficit model and participatory capture, community building appeared to take the material and racial composition of neighborhoods as given rather than as the result of government policy. Thus, in the eyes of HOPE VI, communities were already fully formed as well as distinguished by immutable cultural characteristics. The language of assets facilitated the naturalization of this view.

Ultimately, HUD's actual definition of community is not as telling as its ability to define what community means in justifying and conducting its policies. This ability to define communities—similar to what Foucault termed "governmentality"—allows institutions and organizations to define problems for a targeted group of people and also to define targeted groups of people as problems themselves. Foucault (2007) defined governmentality as "the ensemble formed by the institutions, procedures, analyses, and reflections, calculations and tactics that allow the exercise of this very specific, albeit complex form of power, that has the population as its target" (2007, 108). HUD had as its target population low-income, Black residents of "bad" neighborhoods. From that perspective, "an evaluation of HOPE VI's success depends largely on HUD's definition of community" (Barlieb 2007, 210). Often, HOPE VI managers defined community as the quality of a neighborhood's physical area (property rates and crime reduction statistics, for example). Conversely, if HUD's "community,"

> refers to the residents themselves, then a [privatized redevelopment] model that results in the reduced availability of public housing is problematic. The HOPE

> VI project does not make a large portion of the "community" any better off because the project serves only to displace its members. (Barlieb 2007, 210)

This displacement highlights another core (albeit paradoxical) element of participatory capture—by enlisting societally marginalized participants into a hegemonic, institutional endeavor, the organization undermines the preexisting collective bonds that allow for community resistance and identity. Not surprisingly,

> Public housing communities are hotbeds of social and political activism, a characteristic attributable to an environment conducive to organizing. The propensity for activism is often born out of the shared circumstances and strong social ties among residents and is often fueled by the communication network. (Wolfson 2005, 61)

In contrast, HOPE VI neighborhoods, in particular, resulted in marked dislocation and splintering of local community ties as a result of federal redevelopment. In HOPE VI, "thousands of public housing units were sacrificed and restrictive admissions policies fenced out would-be returnees—including friends and family. . . . Without showing sensitivity to racial composition, it is difficult to maintain powerful social networks that nurture successful communities" (Kost 2012, 1412). Yet, in an instance of participatory capture, HUD's discourse singled out the community social capital at the same time that the organization undermined the social capital's legitimacy by using governmentality to delegitimate the integrity of what HUD defined as problem areas inhabited by problem subjects.

This ability to define spaces and people in need of intervention scaffolds the deficit model of governance. HUD relied on the criminalization and stigmatization of low-income, Black residents to legitimate its policies. HUD wrote,

> The relationships created and nurtured by [existing low-income] community structures become a kind of social capital. . . Community building initiatives that work do so by redirecting the energy of residents away from dependency and a victim mentality toward positive and constructive goals for the wider community. (HUD 1997, 10)

The distinction between dependency and constructiveness formalizes the deficit model—a before-and-after—whereupon the low-income, marginalized residents become more productive with institutional intervention, thus seeming to align the interests of residents with the interests of more powerful stakeholders. This alignment had the added effect of materializing the geospatial populace being called upon (i.e., translating the fungible into a body to be acted upon). The body that materialized in HOPE VI's community-building discourse was a body-at-risk that needed institutional rehabilitation—for HUD, the body of public housing was afflicted with (Black) crime and disease. The department argued that, "Health problems, especially chronic conditions, can be one of the biggest stumbling blocks to success, especially for minorities" (HUD 1997, 23). Public housing residents suffered from "stress, smoking, poor nutritional habits, lack of access to healthcare, inadequate coping styles, and a general lack of health education" (HUD 1997, 24). At the same time, the conditions for residents were said to have originated with the populace itself, further backing the deficit model. For instance, HUD argued that "Exposure to violence both outside and inside the home has also been identified as both a health risk and a factor leading to long-term physical and emotional or behavioral problems that can form barriers to success" (HUD 1997, 24). By invoking residents' health and homes (i.e., their very social animation) as "barriers to success," HUD implied that residents lacked agency and needed to be managed or sanctioned before they could achieve a fully formed agency. This implication is further underscored when HUD offers that "Social epidemiologists have shown that social ties even have a measurable impact on health and longevity." Yet, according to HOPE VI, public housing residents maintained "comparatively few social and community ties" and "face substantially greater risks of physical and mental illness and mortality" (HUD 1997, 26). This biopolitical function narrowed the scope of what constituted "participation." Having framed the residents within the deficit model, institutional stakeholders were better able to negate any modes of cooperation, democracy, resistance, and development practiced by residents prior to, or later against, intervention.

For HUD's deficit model, community building meant that

> The residents of many public housing neighborhoods often have been isolated from each other and cut off from the larger community and its opportunities. They have been defined as dependent, passive recipients of services, subject to other people's priorities. They have been at the mercy of many forces over which they have no control, such as poor maintenance, drugs, and other criminal activity—much of it the doing of outsiders. (HUD 1997, 13)

HUD also offered that

> Too often they have spent what collective energy they have mustered to work on obtaining basic services or fighting off terribly negative conditions in the "projects." These residents have lacked the means of creating the kind of social capital that binds families to one another and creates access to opportunities. (HUD 1997, 13)

This aspect of participatory capture is iterated in HOPE VI's asset-driven orientation, with regard to what makes a community viable. HUD defined community or group assets as "all those material and human factors that constitute its often underutilized resources" (HUD 1997, 14). HOPE VI's use of the term "assets" encapsulates determinative ironies with respect to participation as flowing from institutionalist imperative. For one, the evaluation of assets functions to map the material value of a community from an interventionist viewpoint. What is deemed an asset to the interventionist becomes a liability to the resident because the "asset" facilitates a divestiture of power—it reduces agency. In fact, the imperative "Begin each community's strategy with an inventory of its assets" was among HUD's "Successful community-building activities" (HUD 1997, 14). These "underutilized resources" imply that residents themselves lack the capacity to "utilize" their own resources. Accordingly, the extent to which community resources actually function as resources appears limited in HOPE VI's community-building framework, illustrating once more how participation can become an organizational operation in capture.

Resident Councils and Their Roles in Legitimating Participation

Participatory capture can occur when institutional, top-down directives inherently figure participation as a framework for reducing and eliding conflict among structural adversaries. HOPE VI's community building heavily emphasized governance, or the coordination of stakeholders through official, formal organizations. In this regard, the discourse of participation allowed for the introduction and empowerment of myriad stakeholders, not just housing residents. Vale (2019) calls this framework "constellation governance" and argues that HOPE VI's structure lacked uniformity and instead represented "constellations of forces," which included "the housing authority, the housing market, the local political climate, the power of neighborhood groups, the strength of tenant advocacy organizations, and neighborhood experience with prior urban renewal efforts" (2019, 24). Resident councils were also a part of the governing constellation. While resident councils have become standard policy methods for engaging housing residents, HOPE VI's organizational approach reveals that councils can be framed as participatory even as they work against their participants. In this section, I articulate the governance model, wherein more formalized organizational entities splintered the collective potential for resistance in favor of the federal government but not necessarily on behalf of the most vulnerable residents. HOPE VI's community building relied on a static model of deliberation. On the surface, it appears that HUD embraced a representative system, wherein resident councils spoke for those living in the buildings or communities in question. While councils are common practice in housing development, HUD seemed to understand councils as a method mostly to reduce conflict and friction with (and not necessarily among) residents. The Department's utilitarian embrace of councils reflects the chronic, uneven distribution of power inherent in development, further troubling the efficacy of participation in such contexts. Moreover, vague, noncommittal discourse paid lip service to proposed participatory ideals while still leaving in place hierarchical power dynamics that ultimately reduced democratic resistance to HUD's housing developments.

In HOPE VI, HUD took the stance that "Resident involvement is typically centered in an elected resident council" (HUD 1997, 66). The Department advised, "The housing agency should take steps to ensure that the resident council is truly representative of the community" (HUD 1997, 66). Meanwhile, HUD required "that all affected residents be given reasonable notice of all meetings concerned with HOPE VI planning and implementation and that they be given adequate opportunities to offer input" (HUD 1997, 66). Beyond the resident council, other methods of engagement, or what HUD termed "opportunities to participate," included "holding open meetings, conducting resident surveys, and providing technical and leadership training to interested residents" (HUD 1997, 66). Meetings, training, and surveys are standard methods for engaging stakeholders in planning processes. And HUD mandated that public housing authorities consult with public housing residents in drafting their initial redevelopment proposals. These consultations ideally took the form of "a resident training session and several public meetings" (Vale 2019, 27). However, these requirements

> remained vague, so actual practices varied quite a bit. . . . [and] participation could often be rather rushed and limited, especially if a local tenant organization had leaders who were not broadly supported or well engaged with the full range of constituencies in the development. (Vale 2019, 27)

In this way, participation often became non-participatory, creating a crowding-out effect that amounted to something more akin to collusion among more powerful stakeholders. Likewise, HOPE VI embraced an antagonistic stance in which these planning engagements served to manage the risk of resident pushback and stakeholder conflict.

For example, HUD advised that "The housing authority must also help residents to contact a legal aid attorney and any other consultants they wish to have present at these meetings" (HUD 1997, 66). Additionally, they advised "that residents get involved and line up technical advisors at the very beginning of the process so they will be prepared to grapple with and respond in an informed manner to each set of decisions that need to be made" (HUD 1997,

66). At the same time, HUD maintained that decision-making capacity lay primarily, if not solely, with more powerful stakeholders. The Department wrote,

> The housing authority has final decision-making authority regarding HOPE VI funds, but it is imperative for the sake of the ongoing relationship that the input and cooperation of residents be sought before any significant changes, such as demolition or major planning studies, are authorized. (HUD 1997, 66)

In referencing the temperamental nature of the "ongoing relationship," HUD acknowledged the adversarial conditions among the process's stakeholders. But, in perpetuating its institutionalist ethos, HUD iterates its preference for approved organizational action. Indeed, the prospect of agency among residents is what HOPE VI sought to avoid. In touting its training program, HUD suggested that "A leadership training program provider, such as a local community college or civic organization, may carry out the training program for resident representatives" (HUD 1997, 66). The department also turns back to the resident council as the standard governance model and offers that "Working together, the housing authority and the resident council should set both long- and short-term goals, with benchmarks for evaluating success. Resident leaders should strive for a sense of order and purpose at all meetings" (HUD 1999, 66). This bias toward organizations and institutions reflects HOPE VI's participatory capture, which privileged resident displacement in favor of representative voices amenable to HUD's and developers' priorities.

On this front, HOPE VI sought to manufacture the appearance of consent. In reference to its position on resident councils, HUD wrote that "The resident council should build a new spirit of cooperation among all the residents and urge them to lay aside old disappointments and resentments and move forward to a new relationship with management" (HUD 1997, 66). Once more, HUD openly acknowledged an adversarial relationship but turned to participation in seeking consent, concluding that "Constantly bringing up old promises that were not kept . . . only gets in the way of new business and perpetuates negative feelings" (HUD 1997, 66). In prioritizing resident councils, HOPE VI attempted to recruit participants to align with institutional agendas, further demonstrating that participatory methods and their attendant discourses maintain a precarious relation to capture. In participatory capture, participation is a rhetoric and methodization of sovereignty insofar as it seeks to preserve institutional means and logics. Foucault comments that sovereignty is

> not a matter of imposing a law . . . but of the disposition of things, that is to say, of employing tactics rather than laws, or, of as far as possible employing laws

> as tactics; arranging things so that this or that end may be achieved through a certain number of means. (2007, 99)

In HOPE VI, HUD relied on the governance of resident councils in conjunction with rhetorical appeals to the inherent deficit of low-income Black residents to arrange development projects in ways that limited residents' means of democratic resistance and community-building.

Meanwhile, if the sovereign is that which "decides on the exception," as is commonly argued in critical analyses of state and legal power, participation can be construed also as maintaining sovereignty at the expense of a population constructed as or as part of the exception. For HOPE VI, the exception comprised the racialized dysfunction associated with low-income U.S. housing. While racialized hierarchy had become normalized in U.S. public policy and cultural discourse, the ideological persistence (and socioeconomic effects) of said hierarchy is often invoked to legitimate institutional intervention as was the case in HOPE VI. As previously mentioned, residents in U.S. low-income and public housing were constructed as threats or impurities that imperiled the national body and its juridical-civil order. In this respect, residents were the foundation for the state's authority. As the exception legitimating HOPE VI, residents, their deficits, and their blighted, aberrant conditions constituted the federal government's sovereignty, its raison d'état, and its "moment" to enact its housing agenda. Moreover, the liminal position of residents illustrates that, as a "borderline concept," sovereignty can maintain a zero-sum effect, where in the case of the government and public housing residents, for example, one entity's power is contingent upon the absence of power in another. Thus, participation can become capture by virtue of reification and reiteration of presuppositional hierarchies, often implemented through organizational and institutional discourse. Indeed, "participation" functions rhetorically and methodologically to govern subjects, and participation exemplifies the argument that power is proportional to its ability to conceal itself. Participation epitomizes this ability to hide, thereby signifying organizational discourse strategies that obscure their own power even as they claim to bestow power upon the otherwise "powerless."

CONCLUSION

Participatory capture manifested in two models of housing and economic development: deficit and governance. Deficit models rely on the purported inherent deficiencies in a particular culture or population, while the governance model, in its reliance upon exceptionalism and representation, undermines collective resistance to antagonistic, institutional imperatives. Both models are figured as participatory, though they can work against the interests of the most vulnerable participants, as occurred in HOPE VI. Indeed, HOPE VI's community-building approach often resulted in the dismantling of communities. In the context of HOPE VI, "community" served as the fulcrum of participatory capture by which institutional stakeholders were able to conflate participation and exclusion.

The arguments in this chapter are not wholesale indictments of community organizations, which function as indispensable local resources that often support the needs and interests of vulnerable residents. However, philosophical skepticism and critical interrogation of institutional processes are key aspects that sustain the integrity of community organizations. As Gonzales (2021) notes, "organizational trust is not always a positive force . . . it can be coopted as a mode of control, used to minimize dissent and to socialize members into a homogenous organizational culture" (2021, 18). Conversely, "organizational mistrust, or collective skepticism . . . serves as a tool for safeguarding resident-led planning processes, expanding collaborative organizational networks, building leadership among local residents, and transforming negative perceptions of the neighborhoods in question" (Gonzales 2021, 18). Thus, this chapter can be viewed as an exercise in critically productive skepticism, especially since, while "asset-based redevelopment may seem comprehensive and community-focused, critics of this approach argue that residents are generally not trained in planning processes and can be easily swayed by charismatic politicians and technocrats to vote against their best interests" (Gonzales 2021, 8).

Meanwhile, participatory capture in development contexts is almost always (if not inherently) a racialized phenomenon. Economic development projects, particularly those that are in some way cross-cultural, are often race-based; and racial politics and racialized materiality undermine the efficacy of participation to the extent that universalism itself is understood as an instrument of antiblackness. In HOPE VI and subsequent similar approaches to housing development in the United States,

> tenants are not able to participate throughout the redevelopment process when they are relocated and never return to the development. In particular, the uncertainty over who will be invited back makes it particularly difficult for tenants to meaningfully contribute to the development plan. (Greene 2008, 228)

Given such power dynamics, postcolonial and racialized development assumes both a universal equality and a presupposed inhumanity of difference that legitimate the market's efforts to assimilate the "inhuman" or "subhuman" as a means of enacting Anglo-American transnationality. This argument flows from the dilemma of race (as naturalized difference) as being determinative of equality (to be achieved). Historically, "the stipulation of abstract equality produces white entitlement and black subjection in its promulgation of formal equality [i.e., institutional and organizational policies of meritocratic equality]" (Hartman 1997, 116). Given the persistence of antiblackness in Western institutionality, however, participatory policies and methods can be used to maintain social control.

Participatory approaches cannot override their contexts. In the United States, race (as defined legally and ontologically by property) has been arguably the central arbiter in the housing market and the government's role in it. What iterative powers of raciality, then, does the state and its approved, aligned institutions invoke in recruiting their Others to take part in national projects? In what ways can surreptitious, methodical acknowledgments of exclusion on the part of institutions more effectively undermine resistance to hegemony than gratuitous, spectacular displays of legal, organizational, and institutional power?

Analyzing participatory capture allows scholars and practitioners to consider these questions and how participation for marginalized populations can represent the threshold of Becoming and thereby legitimate any institutional action as long as the structure being participated in remains intact and strengthened. In this regard, understanding difference and exclusion *as* an always-already participation

> allows us to see how racial and cultural differences have . . . been deployed to reconcile a conception of the universal (as encapsulated by the notion of humanity) with a notion of the particular (of difference as marked in bodies and spaces). (Chakravartty & Silva 2012, 370)

In participatory capture, institutions and organizations call upon participants, with the dual, paradoxical assumptions that: (1) participants are outside of (or simply not of) the institution; and yet (2) the institution maintains an inherent, active ability to exercise power over the (non)participant.

Chapter 4

"No Better Place"

Voice, Sovereignty, and Information Design in HOPE VI Newsletters

Choice Neighborhoods (2010–present) is a HUD program that extends the mixed-income model and seeks to redress HOPE VI's displacement effect wherein relocated residents were more likely to experience homelessness and housing instability (Popkin et al. 2004, 21). The program is so named for giving public housing residents the choice of either staying or leaving their current neighborhoods. This "choice," however, is not without complications, especially where resident agency and self-determination are concerned. HUD's offer to residents still leaves current dwellers with little to no say in the direction of their communities or any other neighborhood. In fact, the program, with its own participatory capture, serves to iterate the state's imperative over the conditions of space, property, and the lives of lower-income communities. As a policy initiative, Choice Neighborhoods seeks to move beyond merely rehabilitating distressed public housing sites and instead looks to "transform neighborhoods experiencing economic decline into mixed-income communities with improved schools, local businesses, and attractive neighborhood amenities, such as recreational facilities" (Conte & Li 2013, 24). As a result, while HOPE VI undermined existing residents with displacement and disenfranchisement, Choice Neighborhoods undermines existing residents by pricing them out of gentrifying areas.

As Conte and Li (2013) observe, Choice Neighborhoods, the HOPE VI successor, signifies the "disconnect between the rhetoric of neoliberal housing policies and its actual manifestation [in contributing] to the persistence of concentrated poverty" (2013, 28). While Choice Neighborhoods seeks to mitigate displacement by building around and within economically disadvantaged areas, the program's policies "do not provide long-term safety-net supports, which are essential for residents to ward off the effects of gentrification and benefit from the new neighborhood economy" (Conte & Li 2013, 28).

Choice Neighborhoods maintains various holdovers from HOPE VI, including the desire to leverage public grants to further encourage private financing. Not surprisingly, the federal government justified Choice Neighborhoods by touting the successes of HOPE VI. As one critique noted, in the spirit of HOPE VI,

> Choice Neighborhoods has deliberately targeted neighborhoods with significant redevelopment potential. As in HOPE VI, it provides justifications for urban renewal typical of the neoliberal era, formulated in terms of the enhancement of territorial assets, the development of human capital or public investments that make it possible to save on future expenditure. (Kirszbaum 2019, 3)

In addition to maintaining the mixed-income/gentrifying framework of HOPE VI, Choice Neighborhoods continued the rhetorical and programmatic deployment of participation.

HOPE VI's participation gestured toward more explicit resident involvement in the actual public housing sites themselves. The way participation operates for Choice, however, differs somewhat from the participation of HOPE VI. Choice stipulates that residents additionally should be offered the choice to participate in whatever service or neighborhood development initiative the housing authorities decided for a developing area. As Choice progressed in its early programmatic life, HUD published "Choice Neighborhoods Promising Practice Guides," which detail the prescribed technical assistance models that would meet broad federal expectations for helping residents. One published in 2015 called *This Is Our Community—We're All In: Civic Participation in Pittsburgh's Larimer/East Liberty Choice Neighborhood* is an example of how Choice relied on the governance model of participation (described in chapter 3), in which HUD defines participation largely along institutional lines, despite appeals to localism and empowerment. For example, the practice guide says, "Civic participation can take many forms, from active involvement and leadership in community forums, meetings and planning processes, to advocacy for policy positions, to roles in decision-making bodies" (HUD 2015, 1). In advocating for the governance model of participation, the authors emphasize the caveat of civic participation, which privileges ordained, sanctioned forms of deliberation and representation (i.e., forums, meetings, and planning options). In this regard, HOPE and Choice share the same antecedents for participatory capture. HUD, for instance, specified that "[Choice] Grantee teams that included public housing authorities (PHAs) built on their previous experience implementing services as part of their HOPE VI grants" (HUD 2013, 39). In the end, it seems the only major difference between Choice and HOPE VI is that HOPE VI explicitly displaced residents while Choice offers the option of staying in an increasingly expensive area or leaving.

As seen in the Choice program, the reformulation of neoliberal participatory rhetorics demonstrates the embeddedness of participation's assumptions that institutions can do the most good to help the vulnerable and that, with institutional assistance, the vulnerable can play a significant role in bettering their own conditions. This paradigm, of course, functions to empower institutions often at the expense of the affected who, in performing roles on behalf of institutions, undergo an erosion of sovereignty. In the previous chapter, I mentioned that HOPE VI's participatory capture invokes the concept of sovereignty, because the federal government's vision for communities often clashes with and supersedes the vision many communities have for themselves.

In supporting a more localized, communally informed conception of sovereignty, I see sovereignty, ideally, as a community's ability to exercise its own cultural and political will upon itself. Moreover, in encompassing social capital, sovereignty would also mean the networks, behaviors, forms of knowledge, and ways of life that community members have developed despite, irrespective of, or in response to institutionalism. This chapter and the next chapter seek to understand the extent to which sovereignty could be instantiated within contexts—potential or realized—of participatory capture. To accomplish that goal, I analyze newsletters distributed to HOPE VI/Choice public housing residents by housing authorities. Newsletters are effective artifacts in this regard because they represent the liminality of being both of and apart from institutions. This liminal position is occupied by participants, public housing residents, and technical communicators who often function as translators, interpreters, or interlocutors between institutions and other audiences. Additionally, newsletters can be classified as institutional participatory documents, since the point of newsletters is to provide information that mobilizes subjects to perform participatory tasks.

My archive consists of newsletters produced by the Louisville Metro Housing Authority (LMHA) as part of their developments associated with HOPE VI and Choice Neighborhoods (HOPE VI's programmatic successor). These newsletters represent a unique archival opportunity because Louisville, as one of the more prominent laboratories for both HOPE VI and Choice, represents a signature confluence of public housing, race, and community. The newsletters, which are housed on the Louisville Metro Housing Authority website, were produced under both the HOPE VI and Choice programs; thus, they can provide insight into how participatory discourses may have morphed or remained static.

The HOPE VI/Choice newsletters selected in this chapter represent activities associated with the Park DuValle development, which ran from approximately 1995 to 2003; the Clarksdale development from 2001 to 2005; and the Russell area development, which began around 2015. The newsletters (a total of thirteen) are written and produced primarily by the Louisville Metro Housing Authority, in cooperation with The Community Builders Inc. (a nonprofit real estate developer) and other development associations. Newsletters range from two to six pages. The inaugural issues provide general descriptions of the government programs that support the redevelopments. After the initial issues, the newsletters provide updates on the redevelopment's progress, and they contain descriptions of initiatives, services, and community events offered by government or housing authority programs. These offerings include: "new homeownership opportunities," times and events for Neighborhood Task Force meetings, and community gardens. The Park DuValle newsletters tend to tout the successes of the program, with headlines like "Intergenerational Computer Program A Hit" and "Park DuValle Community Health Center, stronger than ever at 35." Clarksdale's newsletters use more columns and feature profiles. The profiles depict both residents and institutional representatives like the housing authority public information officer. Generally, these profiles personalize programmatic successes and interventions by highlighting how the program's services have made a difference in people's lives. Clarksdale's columns appear to be written by political figures. While Park DuValle's newsletters contain a regular column written by then-Louisville mayor Jerry Abramson, the Clarksdale newsletters additionally host columns by the housing authority executive director and a Louisville councilman. Newsletters written for the Russell redevelopment uptake the profile genre by regularly featuring resident spotlights—small articles that highlight a resident's contribution to the neighborhood.

Aside from these specific documents written as part of the HOPE VI and Choice programs, newsletters represent rhetorical and information-based power struggles between institutions and possible participants. Often, the least powerful stakeholders see information as useful resources in protecting themselves against exploitation and disenfranchisement. In housing, both institutionalists and residents have acknowledged that newsletters serve to keep residents informed and encourage participation. For example, in a study of an integrated residential neighborhood in North Carolina (with "direct implications for federal programs like HOPE VI"), Mayorga (2012), identified the circulation of newsletters as an exercise of power. She writes that "homeowners maintained control of the neighborhood association . . . through . . . advertising practices: (1) the online e-mail listserv and (2) the quarterly newsletter" (2012, 85). At the heart of the exercise was the "importance of newsletters in eliciting participation" (Mayorga 2012, 86). The newsletters were not without issues of power and access. Mayorga found that, "Nonwhite residents were less likely to get the newsletter and were subsequently less likely to be aware of the association, neighborhood events, and, therefore, less likely to participate" (Mayorga 2012, 87). Accordingly, like participation, information design is not an unbiased exercise.

HUD has long identified newsletters as a go-to option in its participatory toolkit. For instance, in a 1979 document called *Resident Participation in the Housing Management Process: Participant's Workbook*, the Department included a section titled, "Newsletters and Handbooks." The authors state, "Newsletters and handbooks can promote resident participation by encouraging their involvement in resident organizations and by gaining their support for management policies" (HUD 1979, 21). HUD defined newsletters as "periodic (at least quarterly) publications that are useful for announcing new management policies, for inviting resident participation in new programs, and for promoting resident participation in, and support for, existing programs on an ongoing basis" (HUD 1979, 21). Interestingly, as HUD gestures toward participation, the Department stipulates that "Though management itself is generally responsible for producing a resident handbook, both residents and managers can publish and distribute a newsletter" (HUD 1979, 21). Even as the handbook charges management with a responsibility to include residents, the positioning of newsletters as the explicit domain of management signals a hierarchical dichotomy between residents and the institutions apparently responsible for the property.

This particular HUD handbook represents just one of many instances wherein planners, designers, and policymakers have turned to newsletters as a participatory design method. For example, in "Participatory Design and Cyclic Improvement of Business Processes with Workflow Management Systems," Hermann and Walter (1997) point to "newsletters as a 'mode of participation' for employees" (1997, para. 8). In "Participation in the Planning and Design of Public Open Space," Heyer (2011) lists newsletters on a comprehensive list of "common participatory design and planning activities" (2011, 31). And in "The Fallacies of Open: Participatory Design, Infrastructuring, and the Pursuit of Radical Possibility," West-Puckett et al. (2018) identify newsletters "written by participant-facilitators" as especially "facilitative . . . [within] design meetings" (2018, 215). Overall, participatory practitioners have used newsletters to facilitate action through information sharing. Moreover, newsletters can provide rhetorical and documentational insight into a neighborhood's activities and cultures, especially when newsletters are understood as organizational tools.

Residents are typically the audiences for newsletters in community-building contexts. Kingsley et al. (1997) indicate that "community associations often . . . regularly distribute newsletters to all neighborhood residents on changing plans, progress, and upcoming events" (1997, 37). From a community-building perspective, the intent is that "the leaders of community-building initiatives remain representative of neighborhood residents as a whole, and that residents retain a high rate of direct participation in the initiative's activities" (Kingsley et al. 1997, 37). HOPE VI officials advised that "The housing authority must develop a public information strategy that provides for regular communication and information sharing with the residents regarding all aspects of the revitalization plan" (HUD 2000, 67). The officials conclude that "a regular HOPE VI newsletter is an effective means of keeping residents (especially those who are temporarily relocated) updated and connected to the revitalization process" (HUD 2000, 67). The point of the newsletters then is to keep residents informed about a community's activities, with the assumption that information design is participatory design, that organizing information helps organize participants.

McKnight and Kretzmann (1990) categorize newsletters as "communications organizations" and argue that "Strong neighborhoods rely heavily on their capacity to exchange information and engage in discussions. Neighborhood newspapers, particularly those controlled by local residents, are invaluable public forums" (1990, 8). Though McKnight and Kretzmann assess newsletters as "less comprehensive media," they still think of them as "relevant to community building" (1990, 8). This chapter examines the extent to which the HOPE VI and Choice newsletters promoted sovereignty, especially since the newsletters occupy a liminal communicative position—the residents are the primary audiences (and the presumed primary beneficiaries), but the newsletters are written and produced by housing authorities. As such, analysis based on the newsletters informs the similarly liminal position of technical and professional communicators by highlighting both the newsletter's institutionalist HOPE VI rhetoric and a rhetoric of sovereignty reflective of the community.

The following analysis is organized by newsletter and thus by neighborhood and time. The first section examines the HOPE VI rhetoric in the newsletters from the Park DuValle and Clarksdale developments. Choice Neighborhoods is a slight public policy shift from HOPE VI, in that Choice places greater emphasis on residents' social connections to their pre-development communities. This emphasis is rhetorically represented in Choice newsletters by resident spotlights and references to design workshops, which I elaborate on in chapter 5. Chapter 5 evaluates the Choice newsletters, compares them to the HOPE VI newsletters, and extracts sovereign design elements from its attempts to evolve from HOPE VI's past. First, however, I'd like to explore the persistence of participatory capture in the HOPE VI newsletters to establish the contrast between participatory capture and sovereign design rhetoric.

HOPE VI Newsletters: Legitimation, Elision, and Exceptionalism

The HOPE VI newsletters for the Park DuValle and Clarksdale developments contained many of the legitimation strategies that predominated in other HOPE VI documents. Importantly, however, the newsletters reveal two additional rhetorical elements. The newsletters featured an elision of resident voice as well as intensified appeals to exceptionalism. The elision of resident voice manifested in how the newsletters' authors used passive constructions to indicate that residents "were pleased," for example, with services provided by the housing authority. The authors in this case, though, rarely used any direct quotations from residents. Meanwhile, exceptionalism was used to contrast "good" and "bad" residents and "good" and "bad" communities. This contrast was used to justify institutional action.

PARK DUVALLE

Park DuValle was one of the earliest and most prototypical HOPE VI developments. Single Black women constituted most Park DuValle residents and represented a statistical success story for HOPE VI interventionist revitalization (Gilderbloom et al. 2005, 11). Prior to the HOPE VI program, the public housing community in Park DuValle consisted of some of the youngest, poorest residents in one of the most crime-ridden areas in the nation (Gilderbloom et al. 2005, 21). Post-HOPE VI, however, analysts concluded that, "Park DuValle Revitalization . . . sparked a surge in middle-class African American homes [with most households being] single African American females" (Gilderbloom et al. 2005, 22). With that pro-interventionist selling point, Park DuValle instantiated at least two major programmatic emphases characteristic of federal neoliberal housing policy: self-sufficiency and affectability. HOPE VI sought "to help families achieve and sustain self-sufficiency, [and to] encourage economic and community investment through employment, education, and human services initiatives" (Gilderbloom et al. 2005, 10). Affectability, the ability of subjects to be affected by hegemonic or institutional action, manifested in the stringent requirements for living at Park DuValle once the newer HOPE VI development was completed. In fact, Park DuValle had "some of the highest standards of personal responsibility requirements in the country; requiring criminal background checks, credit check, rental history check, employment/job training/family self-sufficiency, and housekeeping inspection checks" (Gilderbloom et al. 2005, 10). Rhetoric, however, often flowed in contradiction to lived experience, and HOPE VI's rhetoric of success did not exactly match reality.

As is typical with many federal redevelopment projects, the benefits of intervention are not absolutely discernible. Ten years after the initial HOPE VI grant, Park DuValle was no longer considered a success: "By 2008, the project had not attracted expected levels of new business investment, shopping, and services. More broadly, according to LMHA Executive Director Tim Barry, the project resulted in a net loss of subsidized housing" (Axtell & Tooley 2015, 280). Moreover, "the rhetoric, processes, and results in Louisville disrupted communities, perpetuated disempowerment, and favored deconcentration of poverty over poverty reduction" (Axtell & Tooley 2015, 279). Importantly, however, the processes of the Park DuValle development included the programmatic and rhetorical deployment of participation.

Along those lines, the most prominent rhetorical feature found in the Park DuValle newsletters was the legitimation strategy of participation-as-bio/necropolitics. For HOPE VI, self-sufficiency and exceptionalism signified the healthy, hegemonic norm. This signification is in keeping with the longstanding cultural argument that the poorest (i.e., the most dysfunctional) in society were undeserving of aid or recognition. Accordingly, dependence upon the state (as opposed to self-sufficiency and individual exceptionalism) is figured as an unhealthy threat to the functioning of "normal" society. As described in chapter 2, HOPE VI's overall rhetoric depicted a self-sufficient community sustained by entrepreneurialism and exceptionalism as a properly functioning body. And, for HUD, a self-sufficient community is vital, legitimate, and able to be integrated into the collective whole. This rhetoric set the programmatic stage for a development design that embraced displacement—that is, a design that splintered and displaced low-income communities as a method for economic integration. The irony, perhaps, in gesturing toward participatory capture, is that such displacement measures made obvious the disingenuousness of self-sufficiency—the affected, in this case, were not affecting themselves. Despite the irony, with Park DuValle newsletters, HUD and the LMHA leaned into participation-as-bio/necropolitics by emphasizing the preferability of individual exceptionalism, entrepreneurialism, and self-sufficiency.

Along those lines, notable reference to self-sufficiency comes from one of then-Mayor Jerry Abramson's regularly featured columns. He writes, "Beyond bricks and mortar, there must always be human investment and the belief that if you put forth enough energy, effort and time, good things will come" ("Signs of Progress" 2005). He continues,

> Recently, I rode through the neighborhood, marveling at the homes and watching the children play. I could not help but fondly remember the community meetings and the folks who stood arm-in-arm with the Housing Authority, HUD officials and a host of others, to bring our dream for a new Park DuValle to fruition. ("Signs of Progress" 2005)

In his initial comment, note the value judgment that essentially "good things come to those who work for them." The inverse implication is that "bad things happen to people, because they are lazy or don't work." This sentiment ignores the reality that many low-income people work. It also neglects to speak to non-institutional, sovereign efforts to build and sustain communities. This neglect is echoed in his second comment, wherein he suggests that, without HUD and the housing authority, the community would have continued to languish in dysfunction and would not have achieved "our dream of a new Park DuValle." Once more, the rhetoric falls short of recognizing sovereignty by centralizing success as the result of institutional intervention. Thus, in HOPE VI's figuration, dysfunction is naturalized through depictions of laziness and dependence, a condition cured only through intervention.

In deploying health-based rhetoric, practitioners often use contrasting images of healthy/unhealthy. Common examples are before-and-after weight loss pictures or pictures of white and yellow teeth. HOPE VI used such contrast in participation-as-bio/necropolitics. Specifically, the program used depictions of self-sufficiency and exceptionalism as contrasts to the purported laziness and dysfunction endemic to low-income communities and housing projects. In the Park DuValle newsletters, the housing authority depicted Ulysses Bridgeman as the picture of healthy, exceptional self-sufficiency. Bridgeman was a standout basketball star at the University of Louisville and later in the National Basketball Association. He used his career earnings to eventually become "the second largest Wendy's franchise owner in the world" and acquire a net worth of $400 million (Miller 2017). In reflecting Bridgeman's status as self-sufficient and exceptional (which would make him a desirable figurehead in HOPE VI), one 2017 article wrote, "[Bridgeman's] success is measurable and proactively engaging to all that has seen his progressive growth. He took the hand that was dealt to him and made good choices that resulted in major accomplishments" (Miller 2017). Incidentally, Bridgeman's wife grew up in Park DuValle, and during a Family Day event in Park DuValle covered in one of the newsletters, the couple was "recognized for their outstanding contributions to the Park DuValle community" ("Spotlight on Wendy's" 2005). The contributions identified by LMHA, in this instance, were the role Bridgeman's Wendy's franchises played in supporting various development-related organizations and initiatives.

One newsletter wrote that, "Being involved in the community, especially where he does business is nothing new for Ulysses 'Junior' Bridgeman, president and chief executive of BF South and owner of 153 Wendy's restaurants including the Algonquin Parkway store" ("Spotlight on Wendy's" 2005). The newsletter further details that Bridgeman's company was

> an early partner of the . . . Community Health Project at Park DuValle . . . [whose] mission was to create a healthier, more educated community equipped to address the interrelated problems that prevent residents from achieving their full potential and maintaining self-sufficiency. ("Spotlight on Wendy's" 2005)

Here, the nod to self-sufficiency in pairing with the exceptional is more explicit. Moreover, the intermingling of self-sufficiency and exceptionalism with health is on full display, even despite that one of the main sponsors of the health project is a fast food chain. Nevertheless, the Wendy's partnership led to a Park DuValle "Family Day event . . . sponsored by the Center on Addiction and Substance Abuse at Columbia University. The event promote[d] parental engagement as a simple, effective way to reduce substance abuse among children and teens and raise healthier families" ("Spotlight on Wendy's" 2005). The result was a "first-hand [display of] . . . the positive results of private business partnering with other agencies to better the lives of residents in this community" ("Spotlight on Wendy's" 2005). In this instance, the benevolence of institutional intervention is shown to be the primary cure for the unhealthiness of dysfunctional communities. Dysfunction here means the lack of self-sufficiency and allows for the promotion of exceptionalism, which can undermine sovereignty for low-income communities by facilitating displacement and further intervention.

The exceptionalism attendant toward HOPE VI's use of participation-as-bio/necropolitics stems from the ontology and design domain of neoliberal housing. Specifically, exceptionalism functions as a cultural narrative and reflects longstanding political and rhetorical approaches to public housing. For one, these narratives and approaches have come to reflect mixed-income development methods, which tend to enable institutional negligence of the poorest and most vulnerable residents. Part of this negligence is built into the financing mechanisms for mixed-income developments. Since money for mixed-income properties is raised (through bonds, grants, and tax credits to developers) rather than primarily allocated through public funding, the newer developments are not required to prioritize the poorest. Instead, developers and housing authorities are encouraged to prioritize residents of higher income and to retain them with rent ceilings. This approach was codified in the 1998 Quality Housing and Work Responsibility Act, which generally made work a requirement for entry to subsidized housing.

This requirement meant housing authorities were encouraged "to skip over those with the lowest incomes to reach higher-income working families (who could still be deemed 'public housing eligible' as long as they earned no more than 80 percent of the area's median income)" (Vale 2013, 27). The policy intent in this regard was to "restore as much public housing as possible to the sorts of selectivity and tenant composition that had prevailed at the time of the initial public housing experiment in social relations" (Vale 2013, 27). Such selectivity (i.e., exceptionalism) has long been a desired feature of public housing. Based upon this desire, "much of the history of public housing in the United States has followed a cyclical practice of displacement and neighborhood renewal, frequently directed at purging the poorest from the communities being redeveloped" (Vale 2013, 3). With this perspective in mind, LMHA used the HOPE VI newsletters to promote the Park DuValle development as exceptional and thus as worthy to participate in the national body.

One newsletter article featured the following headline: "Honoring a Model Community and Those Who Are Models for Our Children." The article cites "the privilege of working with the federal government and the Housing Authority of Louisville on a roadmap for rebuilding one of our community's most important and historic neighborhoods" ("Honoring a Model Community" 2003). According to the article author Mayor Abramson, the result of cooperation with HUD was that "Park DuValle is recognized both nationally and locally as a model neighborhood—an example of what can be accomplished when everyone works together toward a common goal for the common good of an entire community" ("Honoring a Model Community" 2003). Here, Abramson ensures that the "model" neighborhood is the result of institutionalism rather than the explicit social capital fostered by the community itself. This reading is supported by Abramson's argument that Park DuValle "has been transformed from a once impoverished and troubled area into a national model of mixed-income housing" ("Honoring a Model Community" 2003). The bio/necropolitical framing remains at work, as Abramson deploys the language of rehabilitation, reclamation, and healing. Notably, he goes one step further and depicts Park DuValle as exceptional for having been rehabilitated or "revitalized."

In a later newsletter, Abramson writes, "Neighborhood revitalization is one area where Louisville continues to shine. I'm proud to look back to when, in 1995, I worked with the federal government and what was then the Housing Authority of Louisville to develop a roadmap for rebuilding one of our community's most important and historic neighborhoods" ("Moving Forward" 2004). Abramson then pivots and embraces Park DuValle with greater use of collective possessives. He writes, "we should recommit ourselves towards meeting our ambitious community goals to transform neighborhoods and the lives of our citizens." He continues, "There's still work to be done. That work is continuing at Park DuValle, which is still growing and evolving into a neighborhood that offers great housing options and the services and amenities that families look for in a community" ("Moving Forward" 2004). According to this rhetorical framing, Park DuValle (having been put to work), is functioning properly, is "evolving," and thus can be recognized as "exceptional" and as a part of the national body.

Not surprisingly, the use of the exceptional is formulated against a backdrop of collective dysfunction endemic to ethnic and behavioral categories. Abramson's appeals to the exceptional and the "common good" take on a racialized character as, at one point in the newsletter cycle, he offers that "just as an African proverb reminds us that it takes a village to raise a child, it's important to show children of all races that there are numerous examples of African-Americans who had a tremendously positive impact on this community" ("Honoring a Model Community" 2003). At the same time, the newsletter touts a reduction in crime in the area: "Compared with the same dates last year, reported crime in the 4th District for the period of Jan 1–Mar 25 for 2003 was significantly down: Property Crime: down 62.5% from 2002 [. . .] Violent Crime: down 60.4% from 2002" ("4th District" 2003). Moreover, in an apparent foreshadowing of the institutionalist view orienting toward the surrounding area rather than on one housing development, the newsletter indicates that "The 4th District covers much more than Park DuValle. It covers the area south of Broadway to Algonquin Parkway, and from 7th Street west to approx. 44th Street" ("4th District" 2003). The incorporation of the larger area within the development project would become a key feature in the Choice Neighborhood program, which justified its approach by arguing that public housing would benefit from area rather than unit redevelopment. HUD acknowledged, however, that this approach tended to minimize resident input (HUD 2000).

Participation-as-Diversity Marketing was another legitimation strategy deployed in the Park DuValle newsletters. This rhetorical strategy depicts participatory approaches as new and cutting edge, and the effect of such a strategy is to position institutions as enlightened. HUD and its housing authority partners were able to gain the upper hand in rhetorical practice by continuously pushing their approach as the best, the smartest, and the most developed. The Park DuValle newsletters promulgate this strategy by emphasizing the "inclusive" character of their programmatic and planning methods. The result is a diffusion or a deflection away from truly local frameworks and away from sovereignty and social capital.

One of the earlier newsletters, for example, touted the formation of the Park DuValle neighborhood association. LMHA wrote, "The Association includes tenants, homeowners, business owners, service providers, churches, schools and community organizations" ("Park DuValle Association" 2003). The same article continued that "Residents are excited about the new sense of community the Association has inspired. Cora Washburn, a Colonial Homes resident for nearly 40 years, is excited about the inclusive nature of the Association. . . . 'Everyone is welcome' [she said]" ("Park DuValle Association" 2003). While one could argue that these organizations represent the truly local character of the community, actual localism here is diffused and obscured. For instance, what role and what social capital do each of these organizations bring to bear on the direction of the development? To what extent do these organizations represent the sovereignty or will of residents? These questions go unanswered; and, indeed, in the rhetorical schema of neoliberal participation, such questions are suppressed, because the assumption is that institutional representation is the equivalent of "voice."

The emphasis on organizational diversity as preferred and innovative plays a central role in legitimation for HOPE VI. Namely, councils and committees function as nominal decision-makers and points of contact for larger institutional stakeholders. While this can increase the institutional functionality of housing developments, it can also lead to a crowding-out effect where only certain voices are prioritized over others. The Park DuValle newsletters engage the legitimation strategy of participation-as-diversity marketing by privileging the plurality of stakeholders and the institutionalization of social capital. This negative effect appears counteracted by the newsletter's use of a quotation from a community member: "Everyone is welcome." On the other hand, a critical framework might reread the positioning of the quote as "Everyone is welcome to join this particular body and participate according to its expectations."

These particular "expectations" call to mind normative, legalistic functions, which can be understood as HOPE VI's legal and programmatic divestitures. From this perspective, the institutional rules of engagement can exclude large groups of residents who are not familiar with certain rules, documents, or processes. The acute legalistic framework was evidenced by the following narrative of the Park DuValle neighborhood association featured in an early newsletter:

> Association board members were elected during a March meeting. One-third of the members will serve until 2004, one third will serve until 2005 and one-third will serve until 2006. Articles of Incorporation were filed with and approved by the Secretary of State, and by-laws were unanimously approved by the Board of Directors. At its March 26 meeting, the board elected the Executive Committee including officers and two members at large. ("Park DuValle Association" 2003)

At stake in the rhetoric of the HOPE VI newsletters is the sovereignty of the communities in question. The assumption is that a rhetoric that at least gestures toward or promotes sovereignty is one that at least highlights social capital. A non-sovereign rhetoric (i.e., a rhetoric of participatory capture) is one that suppresses, ignores, or displaces the value of social capital in favor of privileging institutional interventionism. Often, the HOPE VI newsletters relied upon this type of institutional legitimation.

Perhaps most frequently, the newsletters' rhetorical neglect of sovereignty comes about by the elision of residents as primary actors in their lives and in their communities' development. One article about the "third annual Park DuValle Holiday Festival and Home Tours," for instance, highlights the work of the planning committee without naming or contextualizing the actual committee. In describing the event, the authors write,

> The crowd was down from the 1,000-plus participants last year but everyone seemed excited. The special events committee had been planning since January and hosted a great array of events for young and old alike. Mother Nature cooperated by covering the event with a white blanket of snow that fell all day but didn't dampen the enthusiasm of this year's participants. ("Home for the Holidays" 2004)

The article mentions the participants' enthusiasm but does not quote any of the participants. Meanwhile, in an instance of participation-as-diversity marketing, the article does highlight the myriad organizational actors involved:

> The . . . festival began with a mini-parade or "Holiday Stroll." The parade contingency was small but included Louisville Metro Police and Fire Departments, the River City Drum Corps, Park DuValle area youths, the old-fashion TARC trolleys, Home Depot's mascot and Santa. ("Home for the Holidays" 2004)

The festival is depicted as a continual, popular neighborhood tradition; yet, the article offers no perspective from actual community members.

The persistent lack of sovereign voice suggests that these HOPE VI newsletters are outwardly facing—toward the community rather than produced by it for the community's benefit. This rhetorical orientation is consistent with newsletters as presentations of information. In the context of HOPE VI, residents were presumably meant to activate the information on their own accords. From that view, then, who was presenting the information, and why, becomes imperative to evaluating the discourse at work. On that front, the newsletters, even as they sought to disseminate information, appear to have been written to legitimate and activate the benevolence of institutions and their partners. One 2004 article, for example, functioned as an advertisement for Home Depot, which was "conducting home improvement clinics right here in the neighborhood, and they're open to all homeowners or anyone just interested in learning some home improvement skills" ("Home Depot" 2004). The clinics were arranged by the "Director of Community Outreach and Homeowner Services with the Louisville Real Estate Development Co." ("Home Depot" 2004). The article does not discuss the sovereign will or capacity for homeownership or home repair.

The elision of resident agency appeared in at least two categories: youth and crime. The rhetorical concern for these categories perhaps reflects the concerns about youth and crime that, for policymakers, characterized Park DuValle public housing. Another explanation could be that single mothers comprised a significant public housing constituency. Accordingly, the elision of agency as a rhetorical tactic may have been intended to convince readers that the development was successful in solving chronic issues. Youth development is one of the major areas wherein the institutional was privileged. However, one DuValle article touted the viability of a local education center: "The DuValle Education Center has also shifted and realigned programs and services to meet the changing needs of the community it serves" ("DuValle Education Center" 2003). The authors iterate that

> Since the early summer of 1986, thousands of community residents from infants to seniors have enrolled in programs and received services through the DuValle Education Center. If you're ready to make changes in your life, visit the DuValle Education Center where staff can help you assess your options as you create a new future. ("DuValle Education Center" 2003)

A sovereign orientation, however, might seek to communicate how residents themselves have met their own changing needs or made changes in their own lives. Moreover, in acknowledging the clear necessity for community services like the education center, a rhetoric of sovereignty might highlight the influence that a neighborhood's social capital has had on the direction of the services.

A later article listed the parameters of a Youth Individual Development Accounts (YIDA) program established by LMHA. The mission of the YIDA program was "to assist youth in developing financial understanding and skills early in life" ("Park DuValle Youth" 2004). The article highlights that "YIDA is a partnership between the Louisville Metro Housing Authority, the Center for Women and Families and The Community Builders. The program provides individual development account training and opportunities for community service" ("Park DuValle Youth" 2004). The program mandates a savings plan and the completion of a financial literacy workshop. The privileging of institutional actors, as well as institutional stipulations in the article, render the program participants non-agential while also naturalizing the presumptions behind the institutional imperative to intervene. While it makes sense to list the requirements for participation in a program, the evaluative concern for the sovereign voice might note the construction of the institutional partnership as provider as well as the participants having to meet stipulations in order to receive the provisions of institutional benevolence. This rhetorical construction is an instance wherein resident participation (e.g., in this YIDA program) is iterated within institutional rather than sovereign purview.

Crime and policing are other areas wherein participation is iterated within the institutional. In an article about police-community relations, the authors write that

> The police continue to work diligently in the Park DuValle area and encourage residents to get involved in keeping the community the safe place to live that it is today. Representatives from Fourth District regularly attend Park DuValle Association meetings and residents have been very helpful with calling in information that assist police in doing a better job. ("4th District" 2003)

Though the article mentions the Park DuValle Association and gestures toward resident action, the article contains only a quotation from a police sergeant and does not provide any demonstration of community-led efforts or any voices from the actual community about crime. One possible gesture toward resident action indicates that "Efforts are currently underway to increase the number of neighborhood Block Watch clubs. An organizational meeting is planned on July 21, 6:00 p.m. in the Club House" ("4th District" 2003). The prioritization of the organizational and the institutional, however, remains.

Additionally, when resident voices are featured in the articles about crime, they are used to validate institutional benevolence. For instance, one article noted that "Officers and staff recently returned to the substation on Bohne Avenue at 34th Street. The building had been vacant while a crew worked to alleviate a problem with mold. Many residents are pleased and excited to see the officers return" ("Welcome Back 'Blue'" 2004). The same article features a quote from a resident that reads, "We have a good relationship with district officers. Not only does their presence deter crime but they are good corporate citizens and great supporters of this community" ("Welcome Back 'Blue'" 2004). At the same time, the privileging of the institutional persists. Rather than highlighting any causes of persistent crime or outlining specific strategies to address the issue of crime (considering the necessity and benevolence of the police Department), the article informs readers that

> The Louisville Metro Police Department, under the direction of Major Darice Wiley, has formed a 4th District Advisory Board to address citizen concerns from crime-related issues to abandoned houses. Advisory board members will work on developing solutions to problems affecting the entire community. ("Welcome Back 'Blue'" 2004)

The seeming contradiction between depictions of residents-as-essential resources and residents-as-insufficient in solving community issues is characteristic of the participatory rhetoric of HOPE VI. As noted previously, the elision of resident agency lies at the heart of HOPE VI's argumentative backing. The lack of agency centralizes institutional power to act while also legitimating institutional intervention. Moreover, legitimation in the themes of youth development and crime appears to be downstream from the bio/necropolitical positioning of life and death. Participatory legitimation strategies certainly operate in opposition to rhetorics of sovereignty. The displacement of resident voices (the voices of the affected) in exercising agency is an effective rhetorical framing of participation deployed by institutions. The next section explores how self-sufficiency and exceptionalism functioned to displace resident voices and to delimit resident agency in the Clarksdale development.

CLARKSDALE

After Park DuValle, the housing authority turned its attention to Clarksdale, Louisville's oldest housing project. In the earlier part of the twentieth century, Clarksdale was a white, working-class neighborhood. However, "After Kentucky's 1966 Civil Rights Statute and the nation's 1968 Fair Housing Act, African Americans moved into Clarksdale and Whites fled to other areas of the city" (Axtell & Tooley 2015, 283). Nevertheless, "Clarksdale became a vibrant Black neighborhood, but many businesses closed and some churches joined the flight to the suburbs" (Axtell & Tooley 2015, 283). This flight from the cities resulted in the concentration of poverty and neglect that came to define the inner cities. Decades later, after the Park DuValle redevelopment, Clarksdale was ripe for a similar intervention. This intervention was based on the location of the neighborhood, which sat "by the University of Louisville Medical Center, Jewish Hospital, Louisville Slugger Field, Waterfront Park, and the East Market business corridor" (Axtell & Tooley 2015, 297). The systemic issues that had come to grip the neighborhood imperiled the economic value of the surrounding area.

As a result of this perceived threat, Clarksdale underwent a $250 million redevelopment that was anchored by a "rhetoric of community [which]. . . did not adequately account for existing social capital before relocation" (Axtell & Tooley 2015, 287). Ultimately, rhetoric deployed by HUD and its partners "led residents to believe promises of better lives in a revitalized community, but new housing configurations on the site precluded return for most, new application criteria excluded many, and relocation processes left residents disconnected from prior relational networks" (Axtell & Tooley 2015, 296). In Park DuValle, exceptionalism connoted healthy functionalism and operated as the desired contrast to dependence. With the Clarksdale development, exceptionalism served also to demonstrate the ability of the state to rehabilitate spaces and people deemed unfit or unhealthy.

This demonstrative application further legitimated institutional action, since exceptions were presented as evidence that HOPE VI worked and should be empowered in its mandate. Park DuValle was the exception that legitimated Clarksdale. An early Clarksdale newsletter said the newer development was "modeled on the award-winning Park DuValle neighborhood in Louisville's West End" ("Louisville Receives" 2003). In that same article, however, praise for the revitalization project approval is given to institutionalists, with Mayor Abramson arguing that "Being awarded this grant is the direct result of Representative Northup's leadership, a compelling proposal from the Housing Authority, and a proven track record with Park DuValle" ("Louisville Receives" 2003). Abramson, then, pivots to the contradiction between depictions of residents-as-essential resources and residents-as-insufficient in solving community issues.

He writes,

> success would not have been possible without the involvement of, and support from, Clarksdale residents and neighborhood leaders. And it would not have been possible without the proven record of success that this community has consistently delivered on neighborhood revitalization efforts. ("Dreaming Big" 2003)

Abramson further praises Park DuValle for transforming "one of the most impoverished areas of our community into a neighborhood of pride and a national model for mixed-income housing" ("Dreaming Big" 2003). Meanwhile, the then-housing authority director penned a letter in which he praised an "important element to our success: partnerships and collaborations beginning first and foremost with the residents" ("Partnership" 2003). He notes,

> Much of the Clarksdale revitalization plan reflects what residents told us they wanted and needed in housing and in a neighborhood including a strong emphasis on quality, design and construction. Residents have been major partners in the vision and the plan. ("Partnership" 2003)

Later, he implores residents

> to stay involved and informed. Attend your Council meetings, watch for information we will be providing regularly and call if you have questions. We will begin resident interviews very soon to determine your needs and desires, and to help you choose new housing at the proper time. ("Partnership" 2003)

In this instance, exceptionalism is used to justify participation; and, indeed, participation is shown to be exceptional in and of itself. The housing authority director says, "we will depend on all our community partners—most importantly residents—to help us in this process" ("Partnership" 2003). The appeal to participation on the housing authority's part appears to carry programmatic merit, especially if readers view the appeal as an acknowledgment of the value of social capital. At the same time, the voice of the newsletter remains outward-facing toward residents. That, as well as the call to participate, can be deemed captive rather than sovereign. The call to participate also provides a predicate for a prescribed, predetermined course of action for both residents and development partners.

This programmatic predetermination, anchored by assumptions embedded within participation and exceptionalism, paves the way for the elision of the affected voice. For instance, an early Clarksdale newsletter details the participatory process as follows:

> In July, LMHA staff began conducting interviews with the Clarksdale residents who will be impacted by the first phase of the revitalization effort. During the interviews, LMHA staff are reviewing the relocation process and procedures, and discussing the various housing options and relocation opportunities that will be made available to residents prior to demolition and construction. ("Clarksdale Resident" 2003)

In outlining the participatory process, the newsletter authors offer no mention of the residents' own adjustment to the revitalization effort, despite the nod to interviews and the direct impact of development on residents. Instead, the authors' decontextualization naturalizes the steps taken by institutional partners.

In fact, newsletters used participation to depict the revitalization effort as primarily dependent upon institutional actors. The timeline for the development begins with a "first official site visit since the HOPE VI grant award [by] HUD officials [who] recently met with Clarksdale residents at the East Louisville Community Center and urged them to continue to participate in the revitalization process" ("HUD Officials" 2003). Meanwhile, "This official HUD site visit was required to begin the first steps of revitalization" ("HUD Officials" 2003). At the actual meeting with Clarksdale residents, a HUD technical advisor said, "This neighborhood transformation is 'all about you,' . . . while explaining the various opportunities residents can take advantage of to stay involved and informed as the HOPE VI process moves forward" ("HUD Officials" 2003). The advisor punctuated his remarks by telling residents, "This is an opportunity to think about what you want and work to accomplish it" ("HUD Officials" 2003). Here, the advisor turns to the language of work and self-sufficiency that evokes the bio/necropolitical character of participation.

The legitimation of Clarksdale sometimes used the self-sufficiency paradigm to discuss residents. The combination of this paradigm with the suggestion of exceptionalism contributed to the elision of resident voice in a different way, since a direct reference to specific residents may be taken as an explicit alignment of resident and institutional values. In one article, the newsletter spotlighted "Deandra Adams, a 22-year-old Clarksdale resident, [who] not only gained construction and trade skills, [but] also successfully obtained her GED" ("Building a New Life" 2004). Further emphasizing Deandra's participatory credentials, the authors write, "Deandra is excited about participating in this community-building project for youth in the Clarksdale and Sheppard Square neighborhoods" ("Building a New Life" 2004). At the same time, the newsletter is sure to highlight the intimacy of the resident's reformist, participatory buy-in to institutional benevolence. The authors say, "After graduating from YouthBuild, Deandra hopes to attend college to earn a degree in Human Resources. She also would like to live in one of the homes YouthBuild is currently renovating" ("Building a New Life" 2004). Importantly, the newsletter returns to the bio/necropolitical prioritization of youth development in contextualizing the resident's exceptionalism. The article states that "Although Deandra has a variety of responsibilities and personal goals, her role as mother to her two small children comes first. 'They are the most important people in my life, my focus is on improving our lives'" ("Building a New Life" 2004). While parenting and social support are obviously positive motivations, the rhetorical construction of participation as applied to these categories prioritizes self-sufficiency, institutional benevolence, and individual initiative.

Similarly, the authors of the newsletters are sure to highlight programmatic work requirements. The purpose, in this case, may stem from cultural concerns about the undeserving poor receiving undue assistance. With these concerns in mind, the emphasis on work and initiative (and by extension, exceptionalism) functions to combat skepticism about public assistance and further legitimate institutional action. Returning to the YouthBuild program, the same newsletter detailed that

> YouthBuild Louisville is an education and job-training program for young people ages 17 to 24. While in the program, YouthBuild members participate in leadership development activities, receive social services support, and take college courses in construction and carpentry at Jefferson Technical College. ("Building a New Life" 2004)

The program is validated with requirements, in which participants must work for their value. Namely,

> YouthBuild also helps its young people prepare to receive a GED or enroll in college. Each participant receives a $100 weekly stipend to help defray living costs, and those who complete 900 hours of community service also receive

> a $2,340 college scholarship from the AmeriCorps national service program. ("Building a New Life" 2004)

The stipulative construction of the YouthBuild article is similar to the same construction of the Park DuValle Youth IDA, in which participation is institutionally iterated.

Importantly, this rhetorical iteration within the newsletters follows from the HOPE VI rhetorical framework, wherein the institutionalization of information means institutionalization of design. The HOPE VI framework manifests in the relationship between the rhetoric of the newsletters and the participatory methods enacted in the development. Among those methods were resident/neighborhood councils, whose effectiveness in fostering resident participation is largely mixed. Chenault (2015), for example, presents research that, though resident councils are meant to be responsive to tenant concerns, the structural, representative aspects of councils in federal developments lead to disconnects between residents and managers. Her research suggests that resident council "policies were discriminatory . . . and treated residents unequally" (2015, xvi). Moreover, council members "believed the housing authority really had all the control and that council members did not have any control over the communities they were chosen to serve" (Chenault 2015, xvi). In acknowledging the problem of "self-sufficiency" in development orientation, Chenault concludes that "Policies designed to promote and encourage self-sufficiency actually meant more work for the managers, housing authority officials, and community workers, which in turn meant such groups would be unable to help the council" (2015, xvi). Ultimately, resident councils' inconsistency can be tied back to federally mandated council requirements and guidelines that ineffectively account for and support the localism they are designed to promote (Chenault 2015, 99).

On a similar note, the Clarksdale newsletters offer a discursive link between the organization of information and the organization of people. One newsletter wrote about resident council members that "These individuals will serve the needs of Clarksdale residents, making sure to keep them informed of activities and programs within the development. Residents may contact council members with questions or concerns by calling 569-2382" ("Clarksdale Resident Council" 2003). In the same newsletter, then-councilman Willie Bright said, "The purpose of this newsletter is simple, but important. It's intended to provide our community with the best information possible as we move forward" ("A Message from Metro Councilman" 2003). Similarly, the housing authority representative is quoted as saying,

> As the LMHA Public Information Officer, my job is to not only build a network of individuals who will come together to share information about the Clarksdale

> revitalization, but also keep communication channels open throughout the course of the revitalization effort. ("Making It Happen" 2003)

The housing authority information officer says that, for information sharing, "The creation of the Clarksdale HOPE VI Neighborhood Advisory Council is an important first step in this process" ("Making It Happen" 2003). In demonstrating some of the institutionalized inconsistencies of the resident councils, the council itself was

> comprised of individuals who live and work within the area or are involved in some aspect of the revitalization effort. The Council, which will initially meet monthly, will be patterned after a similar community-based group that was developed for the Park DuValle Revitalization. ("Making It Happen" 2003)

Including individuals who are involved in the revitalization effort may offer some benefit for informing the revitalization effort. The inclusion of such people, however, does not necessarily equate to the best interests of residents or other community members who may dissent against the development's direction. In this way, the council appears to be an organizational manifestation of exceptionalism, a potential supported by the reference to Park DuValle and the use of Park DuValle's own exceptionalism to justify the replication of institutional participatory methods.

Exceptionalism serves an additional purpose beyond the general legitimation of institutional methods. Exceptionalism also allows housing authorities to implement standards and requirements for (re)entry to the new developments. These requirements are in line with cultural anxieties about the underserving poor. They stem from developers' desires to avoid disrupting the new properties and neighborhoods with poor, needy, or dysfunctional residents. On the one hand, a column from Mayor Abramson says, "As we move forward, relocating residents in a thoughtful and sensitive manner will continue to be our primary focus. The Housing Authority will do everything in its power to make sure the needs of residents are met" ("Dreams from a New Community" 2004). Yet, on the other hand, the newsletter indicates that "The first actual [Clarksdale] construction will take place off-site, providing new public housing for qualified Clarksdale residents who choose new apartment and single-family rental housing" ("Architects' Work" 2004). The stipulation of "qualified" residents references the reality that many residents were to be displaced, though that same article's headline is "Architects' Work to Meet Resident Needs, Enhance Community." The newsletter highlights a disjuncture, where only certain needs of certain residents are met. The stipulation inherent in the institutional act is assumed to enhance the community, though the definition of community seems to have little input or reflection from the actual residents, since at least some are not meant to return or participate in the development. Furthermore, rhetoric such as this (that defines community beyond the control and scope of actual residents) facilitates the development expansion (i.e., from individual housing site to neighborhood) that HUD acknowledged reduced actual participation.

With that facilitation in mind, the stipulative function and its roots in depictions of exceptionalism expands the purview of institutional affect. Namely, since Park DuValle was considered an exceptional success, the LMHA was further empowered to try their hand at affecting larger, more consequential swaths of land. Abramson in one newsletter, for instance, commemorated the beginning of construction for the Clarksdale development by offering that, "This is our second opportunity in Louisville to completely reinvent a neighborhood and to create an environment that seeks and encourages diversity" ("Clarksdale HOPE VI" 2005). Not surprisingly, he draws from the well of exceptionalism, writing, "We have shown the world how a successful HOPE VI grant can work at Park DuValle, and we are ready to prove we can do it again" ("Clarksdale HOPE VI" 2005). Similarly, then-Congresswoman Anne Northup said,

> This groundbreaking marks the beginning of a long-overdue improvement in the quality of life for Clarksdale residents, and will be a tremendous boost to the overall downtown area. Clarksdale now joins the rest of downtown as a new center of growth and activity in Louisville. ("Clarksdale HOPE VI" 2005)

With Northup's comments, the newsletters deploy rhetorics of both health and cultural narrative, wherein an entire area or city, rather than just one housing development or neighborhood, can be revitalized through institutional measures.

Additionally, the newsletters stress that the bio/necropolitical cultural narrative underpinning institutional participation means integration into the national body. One article argues that, "You make that progress possible by being a part of the important network of neighborhood residents, organizations, businesses, and local, state and federal agencies who are working together to make the Clarksdale HOPE VI revitalization a reality" ("Louisville: A National Leader" 2005). Further invoking a health-based framework, the article continues,

> This new neighborhood is being built as our downtown is growing and thriving, bringing more Louisvillians downtown. The Clarksdale HOPE VI revitalization will not only transform the Clarksdale neighborhood by drawing a mix of individuals and families from all walks of life, it will have a ripple effect of new growth and investment in surrounding areas. ("Louisville: A National Leader" 2005)

The privileging of terms like "growing," "thriving," "revitalization," "walks of life," and "new growth" serves to legitimate intervention; but, the "ripple effect" sweeping throughout the area signifies the assumed expansion of institutional purview.

Lastly, the newsletters' reference to networks should be addressed, especially since the housing authority casts networks as positive outcomes. Despite the newsletters' positive use of the concept of networks, displacement has proven to sever community networks rather than foster them. Additionally, an evaluation of resident councils has shown that the institutionalization of social networks can have a corrosive effect on the efficacy of communal relations. Tellingly, as the new Clarksdale development was coming to fruition, one newsletter article stated, "Over the past few months, Louisville residents have watched as the Clarksdale landscape has changed almost daily. As residents are relocated, block by block buildings are coming down to make way for the new apartments, condominiums, and single family homes" ("Making Way" 2005). The housing authority sought to balance this relocation and displacement with investments into social services (i.e., Community and Supportive Services) for the residents that remained in the neighborhood. These services included "Family Self-Sufficiency, computer education and training, job placement, adult education classes, scholarship programs, and variety of youth resident programs" ("Community and Supportive Services" 2005). In this area, the newsletter wrote, "As the [social services] Case Managers complete the needs assessments for residents in Phase II, they continue to stay in touch with residents who have already been relocated" ("Community and Supportive Services" 2005). One housing authority representative is quoted as saying,

> It's important that these individuals and families know that we're still here to help in any way we can. . . . We want to make sure they are successful in the transition to their new homes and continue to help if any other services are needed to improve their lives. We're committed to our work, and committed to being there for the residents now and in the future. ("Community and Supportive Services" 2005)

The passive construction in "been relocated" reflects the elision of voice and suggests the residents had no choice and had been at the mercy of institutional imperatives. Some may argue that the provision of services (i.e., Community and Supportive Services) signifies an investment in the social capital of residents. That perspective, however, does not account for my own definition of sovereignty, which is comprised of the networks, behaviors, forms of knowledge, and ways of life that community members have developed despite, irrespective of, or in response to institutionalism. Moreover, from a more technical standpoint, it is important to reiterate that social capital tends to erode as a result of displacement.

CONCLUSION

Participatory capture can erode or displace social capital itself, both materially and rhetorically. In HOPE VI, participation functioned as what David Fleming, in *City of Rhetoric: Revitalizing the Public Sphere in Metropolitan America* (2008), called a "discursive habit"—a habit comprising certain rhetorical characteristics (2008, 49). In U.S. housing (and perhaps even in broader development contexts), participation is a rhetorical antinomy, an inherent contraction, meaning that its invocation always implicitly gestures toward a structural irreconcilability.

From that perspective, the logical opposite of participation is destruction—destruction of the system to which subjects can be a party or destruction of the subjects themselves. Otherwise, subjects who are either subjugated or empowered within a system can be said always already to be participants. Thus, when institutions like the U.S. federal government and its agents invoke participation, rhetorically and programmatically, paradigms of subjugation and empowerment are not necessarily altered along more ethical or democratic lines as much as the conditions that sustain such inequitable paradigms to begin with are primed for additional (albeit potentially subtler) rhetorical, material, and libidinal reinforcement.

As a historical case study, HOPE VI reveals participation's antimonic character. For Black Americans living in urban areas, much of the housing (i.e., the ghettoization of American cities) resulted from government policy that explicitly concentrated Black poverty while segregating Black residents from broader housing opportunities. HOPE VI purported to deconcentrate such poverty and segregation by moving residents to other neighborhoods and by inviting new residents into developed areas. Ultimately, the HOPE VI approach led to a reconcentration of poverty and segregation in other areas, as neither the race nor the income levels of displaced residents changed, nor did systemic discrimination against said residents. Fleming, in his own analysis of the HOPE VI-inspired redevelopment of Chicago's Cabrini Green, noted that the participatory processes of the Cabrini Green redevelopment were contentious from the start, but even after the redevelopment was complete, low-income, longtime residents were continually disempowered. Discursively, these residents were framed as "a feature of the neighborhood that comes with the territory" (2008, 141). Conversely, newer, wealthier residents were "consistently described as choice-makers, autonomous agents with the power to determine how they will inhabit the city" (2008, 141). This structural dynamic—of primitive, often dangerous and deviant racialized peoples and spaces on the one hand and white, wealthy, capable civilizers on the other hand—is endemic to the American narrative and was certainly prevalent in HOPE VI and its programmatic successors.

At the same time, structural irreconcilability does not diminish the ways that many struggle against such constraints. Indeed, several scholars, including Fleming, have highlighted cultures of resistance to pernicious institutional narratives and methods surrounding HOPE VI. In combating stereotypes about being welfare queens, drug users, and criminals, low-income Black residents at Cabrini Green, for example, turned to rhetorical appeals that emphasize family, kinship, and Black self-determination (Fleming 2008, 158–176). Cabrini Green's resident management corporation, which largely comprised Black mothers and grandmothers, proposed that one high-rise be converted into a "democratically governed, not-for-profit housing co-op, one of the first such proposals in the history of U.S. housing" (Fleming 2008, 11).

Similarly, Candice Rai, in *Democracy's Lot: Rhetoric, Publics, and the Places of Invention* (2016), also uses Chicago as a prime example of how rhetoric affects housing and urban development. Concerned with vague and suspect tax policies that underwrote acute gentrification in Chicago, Rai notes that city government relied upon "strategic ambiguity" in rhetoric about said tax policy—a policy that, Rai claims, "led to the displacement of thousands of Chicago residents and business owners who were priced out, igniting protests initiated by diverse neighborhood groups, community organizations, and artists" (2016, 22). Moreover, Rai identifies topoi [stock arguments or concepts] commonly used to either oppose or support affordable housing. Among the topoi Rai pinpoints are the "breeding" of poverty and the unfit character of the poor (in opposition to affordable housing) and the need for institutional intervention to ensure a place for everyone in society (in support of affordable housing) (2016, 43–44). Regarding housing approaches like HOPE VI, Rai concludes that

> the introduction of neoliberal housing practices that promote market-driven ideas through rhetorics of democracy and empowerment has led to shifts in the material practices of how affordable and public housing is done, as well as the production of new arguments that make it harder to argue for building more affordable housing while simultaneously strengthening the moral force of opposing arguments. (2016, 63)

I've extended analysis such as Rai's, by identifying participation as an ideologically embedded topos that blurs the distinction between opposition to and support for low-income housing. The effect of participation's ambiguity,

I argue, is to reinforce institutionality and power away from affected resident influence.

Unlike Rai and Fleming, however, this book makes no significant or explicit claims about democracy or publics. Both authors use physical sites—lots, neighborhoods, communities—to demonstrate that rhetoric is not abstract. Instead, for these authors, rhetoric is used differentially depending on context and location. My interest in this book, however, is with participation as a rhetorical trope, a discursive habit, that is iteratively deployed in civic discourses, especially around housing, urban, and economic development. In that respect, I figure participation more as an ideology than as any sort of theoretical or actual arena in which competing interests can be veritably litigated. I'm interested in how those wielding institutional power deploy rhetorics and discourses of participation against affected residents in ways that foreclose or limit the viabilities of public spheres themselves, even as from a technical communication standpoint, genres like newsletters are meant to support at least some public function, namely, to inform residents and to support residents' public involvement.

My perspective, though, is that participation can be used, as was the case in HOPE VI and Choice Neighborhoods, to discredit, elide, or undermine local, democratic, and non-institutional rhetorical practices. The legitimation strategies of participatory capture found in the HOPE VI newsletters signify writing and communication genres as sites themselves wherein differentiated power dynamics play out in public. Conversely, of course, affected residents have found their own methods of communication and contestation that counteract institutional antagonism. As Derek Handley (2019) demonstrated in his analysis of rhetoric in Pittsburgh's urban renewal, "Voices of marginalized communities often had to take new approaches to civic participation as their voices were not often heard or valued when they did speak" (2019, 179). The next chapter considers sovereign design rhetoric as a potential way for writers and technical communicators to more effectively consider marginalized voices.

Chapter 5

Choice, Resident Spotlights, and Steps Toward Sovereign Rhetoric

In the previous chapter, I mentioned that structural irreconcilability does not diminish the ways in which many struggle against such constraints. Of course, recognizing individual, group, and cultural struggles is essential for ethical communication about social issues. Fleming, Rai, and Handley, for example, each highlight cultures of care and resistance in their analyses of urban redevelopment. Indeed, cultures of care can facilitate social capital and instantiate community sovereignty under challenging conditions—a dynamic that hits home for me.

My own great aunt, Devola Benson (affectionately known as Aunt Dee), served as vice president of the citizens council for St. Clair Village in Pittsburgh. St. Clair Village was a public housing project built in the early 1950s. Initially, the project permitted a limited number of Black residents, but white residents' opposition to integration prompted the city to neglect the development, as more Black residents—including some of my family members—moved in. The St. Clair community, despite the project's civic neglect, managed to sustain generations of residents who made the area their home. As a St. Clair community leader, my Aunt Dee provided support and protection: "she helped distribute food to the disadvantaged, pleaded the case of tenants being evicted, passed out Christmas gifts to children and coordinated an after-school program. . . . [and] 'People in the neighborhood looked up to her almost as a mother figure'" (Zlatos 2012). St. Clair Village was eventually targeted for redevelopment under HOPE VI, and hundreds of units were demolished over the course of about a decade. In 2010, the project closed, despite resistance from residents like Aunt Dee: "When they closed down St. Clair Village, knocked the buildings down, fenced it off, it's like they knocked down her heart. They took a piece of her" (Zlatos 2012). Aunt Dee died in 2012. I remember her tough but warm protective nature fondly.

In recognizing the difficulty of losing one's home, it's important for us also to recognize the lives many built and continue to build for themselves and others. As professional writers and technical communicators, how might we enact this recognition?

The following analysis extends the previous chapter's discussion of the HOPE VI newsletters to consider ways that technical communicators can practice or support a rhetorical heuristic that privileges sovereignty over participation. I call this heuristic sovereign design rhetoric (SDR) and define it as a set of rhetorical practices and characteristics that designers, communicators, and audiences use in resisting the inevitability or benevolence of institutional intervention. To recap, I earlier defined sovereignty as a community's ability to exercise its own cultural and political will upon itself. Sovereignty comprises social capital as well as the networks, behaviors, forms of knowledge, and ways of life that community members have developed despite, irrespective of, or in response to institutionalism and capture.

In addition to some of my own family history and experiences, my conceptualization of sovereignty for low-income Black residents in American public housing is informed by theories of governance (and counter-governance) as discussed, for example, in Rifkin's *The Politics of Kinship: Race, Family, Governance* (2024). For Rifkin, sovereignty manifests in the nonnormative methods of community, kinship, and organization that emerge as Black Americans resist oppressive and hegemonic conditions. He establishes sovereignty as the overlooked, "(often gendered) work of creating and sustaining community infrastructures for Black flourishing" (Rifkin 2024, 205). Rifkin additionally concludes that

> Characterizing those formations as political orders can work as a way of refusing the de facto legitimacy of state framings while also drawing attention to the enactment of (explicit or implicit) modes of self-determination by those cast as part of racialized populations. (2024, 209)

Importantly, these modes "are not dependent on state frames" and function as "alternative 'genres of the human'—suggesting other 'horizons' of collective life" (Rifkin 2024, 209). Pittman and Oakley (2018), in their study of Black grandmothers, many affected by HOPE VI, in Chicago public housing, identify similar such modes as "neighborhood-based social support networks" that provided childcare, "word-of-mouth information about neighborhood resources and services," and access to neighborhood organizations (2018, 473). As I analyzed the same HOPE VI newsletters from the last chapter, I read for instances wherein writers rhetorically elevated modes of Black sovereignty.

My method for extricating SDR's set of strategies is based upon my analysis of the newsletters. Tahin (2011) suggests that

> The principal idea behind rhetorical heuristics is that the argument of a speech can only be successful if it can influence or manipulate the way the members of the audience . . . come to a conclusion after balancing the competing probabilities on both sides of a case. (5)

I take up Tahin's idea that heuristics can be generated by implementing opposing viewpoints; and, using the rhetorical criticism and discourse analysis elaborated in chapter 1, I read against the neoliberal, captive rhetorics found in the newsletters. To generate SDR, I practice the same rhetorical criticism as I did in the previous chapters, identify the legitimation strategies within the newsletters, and then articulate SDR as the ideological and rhetorical opposite of neoliberal discourses found in HOPE VI literature. This practice of establishing rhetorical heuristics by reading against the text is a cultural-symbolic response to the compulsions of normative citizenship, which have been deployed against poor, Black, and other affected public housing residents. Given HOPE VI's participatory capture, SDR can be useful in two areas. First, by embracing an anti-institutionalist perspective, SDR is a framework that can help rhetors identify and facilitate the communicative practices of the affected. Second, in SDR, the rhetor's perspective comprises the rhetor's practice. Accordingly, SDR can provide practitioners and educators a way to engage in anti-institutionalism without falsely denying their roles as institutional actors.

SDR has three design pillars (table 5.1): definition, ethos, and rhetoric.I defined SDR as a set of rhetorical practices and characteristics that designers, communicators, and audiences use in resisting the inevitability or benevolence of institutional intervention. A sovereign ethos is the rhetorical positioning of designers, communicators, and audiences as they practice or signify sovereignty. In this case, ethos signifies the perspective of the communicator relative to the community with which they identify in opposition to capture and hegemonic institutionalism. A sovereign rhetoric is specific topoi derived from a sovereign ethos that appear in a communicative design's style, arrangement, and language. In other words, a sovereign rhetoric refers to the rhetorical methods or tools that communicators use in enacting a sovereign ethos. While SDR is a separate framework from the rhetorical criticism I practice on the HOPE VI newsletters, SDR does represent the disidentificatory rhetorical heuristics I articulate in reading against the newsletters' participatory discourse.

Despite the preponderance of participatory capture in the HOPE VI newsletters, there remained some instances wherein the newsletters contained

Table 5.1 Sovereign Design Rhetoric

Design Pillar	*Features/Characteristics*
Definition of *Sovereignty*	The networks, behaviors, forms of knowledge, and ways of life that community members have developed despite, irrespective of, or in response to institutionalism
Sovereign Ethos: the rhetorical positioning of designers, communicators, and audiences as they practice or signify sovereignty	• Prioritizes lived experience • Illustrates historical consciousness • Avoids appeals to exceptionalism • Assumes community ownership without identifying with the inevitability or benevolence of institutions • Understands that the community's social capital has a recursive influence in the process of development rather than linearly or statically in the beginning of development • Demystifies methods • Acknowledges structural oppositions • Features technological and literacy-based accessibility • Makes visible the seemingly invisible • Highlights active stakes in the consequences of the design • Ascribes value to internalized difference
Sovereign Rhetoric: specific topoi derived from a sovereign ethos that appear in a communicative design's style, arrangement, and language	• Rhetorical construction that centralizes the voices of the affected, particularly if those voices are activated in reflecting the value of social capital o Privileging, contextualization, and validation of the perspective of the residents o Personal narratives o Narrative detail o Direct quotations • An identification with the community in opposition to the mainstream o Rhetorical identification practiced by residents o Collaborative phrasing like "share" o Collective possessives like "our" o Nod to the benefits of resident voices across the development's operational spectrum

elements of sovereign design rhetoric. In this case, a sovereign rhetoric centralizes the voices of the affected, particularly if those voices are activated in reflecting the value of social capital. From this perspective, the newsletters that contained or gestured toward a sovereign rhetoric contained also a corresponding design element that too privileged sovereignty. Again, under the assumption that the organization of information influences the organization of people, a sovereign rhetoric equates to a design method that more so prioritizes resident voices. With respect to some instances in HOPE VI, the design method that appears to have gestured toward sovereignty is design workshops that solicited direct input from residents. Further underscoring resident input as a gesture toward sovereignty, the newsletters that centralized affected voices featured "resident spotlights"—articles that introduce neighborhood residents and contain personal backgrounds and opinions. These two elements—design workshops and resident spotlights—are two potentially sovereign rhetorical components that appear somewhat in HOPE VI newsletters but were much more prominent in the Choice program.

DESIGN WORKSHOPS AND RESIDENT ENGAGEMENT

In an early Clarksdale newsletter, the housing authority touted a "design charette (a 'brainstorming' event to discuss design options) . . . to share ideas for renovating and using the old Presbyterian Community Center" ("Use of Donald" 2003). The charette, meant to solicit feedback from residents on neighborhood design, contributes to the demystifying of methods. Meanwhile, phrases like "share" suggest the active validity of the community's social capital, in the sense that the community's social capital has influence in the process of development rather than linearly or statically in the beginning of the development. The demystification of methods is a feature of sovereign ethos, a communicator's rhetorical positioning. I consider demystification a tenet of sovereign ethos because demystification is a counter-framework to HOPE VI's participatory capture, which sought to obscure institutional influence, naturalize institutional intervention, shirk accountability, and suppress resident/community activism. Design workshops, on the other hand, are opportunities for designers and communicators to be transparent; meanwhile, collective phrasing like "share" is a rhetorical prerequisite for identifying with communities.

Moreover, the housing authority supplemented the workshops with individual interviews between residents and the authority's Community and Supportive Services. One newsletter said that "During the interview, CSS staff assesses the family's current status and reviews the support services that will be made available as part of the HOPE VI process" ("Resident Assessments" 2004). The article goes on to say that "The most requested services by residents are employment and educational assistance" ("Resident Assessments" 2004). Meanwhile, the CSS coordinator is quoted as saying, "These interviews give us insight about what programs are working and how case managers can help individuals meet their personal goals" ("Resident Assessments" 2004). Though the article does not contain any direct feedback or quotations from actual residents, the inclusion, contextualization, and validation of the perspective of the residents represent a step toward recognizing social capital. Councilman Bright cosigned the interviews and inclusion of residents, offering, "Clarksdale and area residents have had a significant impact on the design of the neighborhood, on the relocation schedule, and on the community supportive services available to residents. You have made this impact because you have voiced your opinions" ("A Better Day" 2004). The nod to the benefits of resident voices across the development's operational spectrum sheds light on the significance of the affected. Additionally, this nod also represents a rhetorical step toward sovereign ethos by demonstrating that residents have sociocultural value that manifested in their communities before-and-after redevelopment.

The Choice program, as an update to HOPE VI, maintained the overarching appeal to participation and resident voices. One Choice newsletter said that "Community participation is essential to the planning process" and listed several programmatic avenues for engagement. The participatory methods included "community meetings and conversations, participating in task forces, or taking our Vision Russell Neighborhood survey. Task force groups have been formed to focus on each of the four Transformation Plan components—People, Education, Housing and Neighborhood" ("Introducing the Choice" 2015). The engagement campaign could be considered an implicit acknowledgment of the structural opposition at play between residents and developers. At the same time, the engagement methods remained outward-facing and made assumptions about access, literacy, and communal organization. Namely, the engagement was driven by technology and digital tools that may not have been available to all or most residents. In their survey-based outreach, the newsletters primarily directed residents to websites or asked residents to call a number "to speak with someone to get signed up or leave a message with your name, phone number, and your email address and/or mailing address" ("Introducing the Choice" 2015). The effectiveness of the housing authority's approach could also be questioned, given the assumptions at work in the outreach. Later newsletters revealed that a "total of 481 people who live, work or worship in Russell participated in the survey" ("Neighborhood Survey" 2015). Yet, another newsletter would assess that the Russell development affected "nearly 3,800 families" ("A Joint Meeting" 2016). Perhaps the relatively low participation rate for the survey resulted from the outward-facing, institutional direction of the planning effort. A sovereign ethos within SDR, however, encourages communicators and designers to find ways to identify with communities in opposition to institutional, top-down efforts. Thus, SDR would ask, in what ways do my community members conduct outreach and solicit feedback? By taking this identificatory stance with the affected, communicators can demystify methods and move from participation to sovereignty.

RESIDENT SPOTLIGHTS

The Choice newsletters often featured what they termed "resident spotlights"—short articles that highlighted a resident's life and perspective. The articles typically provided the residents' backgrounds and sought also to provide some insight into how the resident was benefiting from housing authority programming. The genre of resident spotlights represents attempts on the part of authors to increase identification between development management and residents. As such, the spotlights contain elements of SDR. Resident spotlights were not new to federal housing; indeed, a similar newsletter feature is found in a Park DuValle newsletter. The newsletter spotlighted the "intergenerational 'My Story' program . . . a shared learning environment for seniors and youth alike" ("Intergenerational" 2005). According to the authors, "Through the use of computers, youth are teaching basic computer and Internet skills to senior residents and, seniors are teaching youth about the life, social and cultural environment of their era" ("Intergenerational" 2005). The program's emphasis on the richness and value of the community members, their lived experiences, and their historical consciousness laid the foundation for furthering the residents' social capital.

By preserving history, the program worked to ensure the future. The newsletter said of "My Story" that "Youth are interviewing area seniors to create and publish their stories on a community web site. 'My Story' may include old photos, which can be digitally preserved and recordings of the senior's voices to publish their story" ("Intergenerational" 2005). With the program's documentary character, the program helped to make visible the seemingly invisible. Lived experiences, historical consciousness, and making visible the seemingly invisible instantiate a sovereign ethos. Lived experiences are the realities that shape residents' identities, values, and communicative practices. In that respect, lived experiences are more accurate depictions of communities than those institutionally or normatively mediated in the mainstream, which can pathologize populations. Historical consciousness has similar significance to communities and, like demystification, can reveal how communities and lived experiences are not inherent or natural. Instead, historical consciousness illustrates how communities—both geospatial and cultural—are often formed as a result of institutional influences ranging from public policy to economic opportunities. At the same time, historical consciousness shows how communities have practiced survival strategies in response to those institutional influences. From that perspective, a sovereign ethos that privileges lived experience and historical consciousness can make visible the seemingly invisible.

The HOPE VI intergenerational spotlight was not without its potential pitfalls. Specifically, some of the rhetoric surrounding the program's legitimation evoked the utilitarianism that framed residents as "assets" in HOPE VI's community building. Additionally, that rhetoric seemed to engage in the same legitimation that sought to ascribe value to residents based upon their capacity to have worked for the support provided to them. The newsletter says about the program that

> In addition to the basics, youth are learning desktop publishing and how to use software and hardware that will prepare them to repair and upgrade their personal computers. Youth are working toward proficiency in at least one Microsoft software program and will test for Microsoft certification after three months. ("Intergenerational" 2005)

On the other hand, the "My Story" article was one of the few Park DuValle newsletters that featured a quotation from a resident. Stanley Dennis of the Dr. William Weathers Senior Building said, "I'm excited. I've wanted to learn about computers but didn't know how to get started. Before long, I'll be able to email family and friends" ("Intergenerational" 2005). However, resident spotlights were rarely used in the Park DuValle newsletters.

Choice newsletters associated with the Russell development, though, reflected consistent efforts to familiarize readers with the outreach workers who were charged with surveying residents about the direction of the neighborhood. Unlike the Park DuValle newsletters, the main characteristic of the resident spotlights was the centering of resident voices with the use of direct quotations and personal narratives. The earliest spotlight introduced outreach worker and Russell resident Jackie Floyd, "[who saw] her work as essential to improving the Russell Community" ("Have You Met" 2015). She self-identifies as "the proud mother of five children, a grandmother of twelve and great grandmother of four [who cares] deeply about our neighborhood's future" ("Have You Met" 2015). Additionally, Floyd is quoted as saying,

> My goal every morning when I wake up is to do something positive that will make our community a better place. . . . The change Vision Russell will bring about is positive for the entire community, both now and for generations to come. ("Have You Met" 2015)

A few discursive aspects of the Floyd spotlight seem to privilege Russell's social capital. First, the outreach worker is an actual resident of the neighborhood under development. That the outreach worker lives in the area conveys that residents have an active stake in the direction of the neighborhood. Floyd's vision for the future further demonstrates resident stakeholding. Secondly, Floyd uses the possessive "our," showing a social ownership as well as social cooperation that has a constitutive effect—it functions as a sort of call-to-action for those who identify with the speaker. This social ownership not only sets the stage for communicators to identify with communities but also provides the rhetorical basis by which communicators can produce counternarratives to hegemonic, normative value systems that pathologize the most vulnerable.

For example, a later resident spotlight extends the identification found in Floyd's profile. This spotlight introduces Mechele Turner, who "loves living in Beecher Terrace. She realizes this might sound strange to many in the community whose opinion of this 76-year-old housing complex is shaped solely by media reports. But for Turner, there's no better place to call home" ("Resident Spotlight: Mechele Turner" 2015). Turner's identification with the Russell area in opposition to what the newsletter frames as an outside misperception reflects an investment in sovereignty. Turner expresses a reality that her community is both apart from the mainstream and of the mainstream. The value ascribed to this internalized difference establishes social capital as a valuable internal resource. In a discursive and ontological framework that figures poor, Black, and minoritarian identities as existing within a deficit, a sovereign rhetoric fosters internal value for one's cultural and social opposition to the hegemonic mainstream. From sociological, political, and rhetorical standpoints, the value ascribed to internalized difference in opposition to institutional violence lays the foundation for positive communal life and checks abuses of power.

Ultimately, Turner's voice becomes a valuable internal resource unto itself, as Turner maintains an identification with the community in opposition to the mainstream. For example, she describes the development's information management as ineffective. She says, "A lot of people in this community don't have access to e-mail or the internet to get information and they are afraid of being pushed out of their home" ("Resident Spotlight: Mechele Turner" 2015). Turner continues, "they are afraid of being pushed out of their home and moved to an area that is unfamiliar. Helping people understand what is being planned is the responsibility of the task forces." The newsletter concludes that

> Turner believes there is much to be proud of in her home. "Beecher Terrace is about families working together and supporting each other. I hope that whatever the group comes up with will enhance what is working and fix what is broken," she added. "I love Beecher Terrace and this is where I want to live." ("Resident Spotlight: Mechele Turner" 2015)

In illustrating a sovereign rhetoric, Turner speaks from the lived perspective of the affected, takes a critical approach to the development's institutional mandates, and advocates for the community's pre- and post-development social capital.

This community advocacy is found in another newsletter about resident Nannie Bibbs, who'd lived in the Russell neighborhood for fifty years. Her resident spotlight reported that "It would bring Nannie great joy to see her neighbors come together and form committees to serve the Russell community. Improving safety and security is part of her vision for the neighborhood, and she sees zoning changes on the horizon" ("Resident Spotlight: Nannie Bibbs" 2016). Nannie is quoted as saying, "We need city planners to listen. . . . We can't just leave change up to our political officials. As residents, we have to do our part" ("Resident Spotlight: Nannie Bibbs" 2016). Nannie's profile evokes a sovereign ethos—one that assumes community ownership without identifying with the inevitability or benevolence of institutions.

From a rhetorical perspective, the sovereign ethos is established, at least partially, by communicating lived experience. One example of the sovereign ethos is a resident spotlight about Pamela Haines, owner of a Russell area restaurant called Sweet Peaches, "a deli-type restaurant where family and friends come together to share special moments, talk politics or just enjoy each other's company" ("Father Daughter Dance" 2016). The article tells the story of how she arranged a Valentine's Day dance for young fathers and their daughters in the neighborhood:

> One day, Haines, or "Peaches" as she is sometimes called by her customers, was curious about several young men who came to her restaurant on a regular basis. She asked them if they had children and all replied they did but don't get to see them much because of "drama" with their children's mothers. Knowing how important it is for fathers to have an active presence in their daughters' lives, and how that relationship affects how their daughters perceive and interact with men, Haines told the young men she was going to throw a Father/Daughter Valentine's Day Dance. ("Father Daughter Dance" 2016)

Haines described that at the event, held at the Kentucky Center for African American Heritage, "Everyone was dressed up and looking good—I've never been in a room with so many beautiful and happy princesses" ("Father Daughter Dance" 2016). This particular profile is unique among the HOPE VI and Choice newsletters because of its narrative detail in establishing the motivations of the residents, the texture of their social relationships, and the ways that residents support each other absent any institutional intervention.

CONCLUSION

A sovereign design rhetoric is meant to move past the traditional participatory framework. The participatory framework, being susceptible to participatory capture, tends to iterate institutionality and elide the structural, underlying power dynamics attendant toward persistent inequities in material conditions and decision-making ability. A sovereign design rhetoric, on the other hand, seeks to make these power dynamics visible and foregrounded within the rhetoric used in design and community engagements. The technical/professional communicator role is not going anywhere, which requires practitioners and educators to continually seek new, more ethical ways to fulfill our often institutional, privileged roles as mediators of literacy and information. The newsletters analyzed in this chapter are institutional documents produced by technical and professional writers with an affected, marginalized audience in mind. Accordingly, the newsletters were primed for examining how rhetoric, even in institutional settings, has the potential to bring about accountability and efficacy by pushing back against the fact of institutionality and the differentiating violence of the mainstream, hegemonic gaze.

The rhetoric and discourses of participatory capture that proliferated in the HOPE VI newsletters served to reinforce hierarchy and affectability, rendering the vulnerable less agential and therefore less resistant. The narratives of community life found in Choice's resident spotlights, however, reorient both the rhetor and the audience away from the norming tendencies of institutional intervention. The design workshops gesture toward the inherent, animating value of a community's social capital (i.e., its sovereignty). Jones and Walton (2018) defined social justice research in technical communication as "investigat[ing] how communication, broadly defined, can amplify the agency of oppressed people—those who are materially, socially, politically, and/or economically under-resourced" (2018, 242). To that end, they argue that "Narrative is an important tool for ethical reasoning because other ethical guides such as heuristics, politics, and principles are necessarily vague and can be difficult to apply to specific ethical dilemmas" (Jones and Walton 2018, 249). Not only does my analysis of the HOPE VI and Choice newsletters offer a specific case study to provide real-world examples of rhetorical consequence, but it also collapses the distinction between narrative and heuristic by offering rhetorical methods with which communicators can tell more ethical stories.

Chapter 6

Implications for Teaching, Public Policy and Engagement, and Future Research

"Participants" are often recruited, studied, and then rhetorically framed by a hegemonic, institutional gaze. In these instances, participants' fates are determined by how technical communicators justify a participatory project's problems, solutions, and stakeholders. Thus, when participation is invoked, power over the marginalized is invoked also, which has the ontological, discursive, and rhetorical effect of asserting power over a marginalized group, resulting in participatory capture. This assertion of power was evident in HOPE VI, a complex institutional effort that rhetorically mobilized participatory discourse within its technical communication. The effect of this mobilization was the further disempowerment of poor, Black, and primarily women residents, despite institutional appeals to agency and self-determination. This discrepancy between appeal and effect signifies participatory capture, which relies upon marginalization to maintain the integrity of normative, mainstream values.

Having analyzed the rhetorics of participatory capture in which participation was leveraged against HOPE VI residents, the corrective framework I've proposed is SDR. I've defined SDR as a set of rhetorical practices and characteristics that designers, communicators, and audiences use in resisting the inevitability or benevolence of institutional intervention. I believe SDR can resist what Tuck (2009) calls damage-centered research, which she describes as "research strategy that frames entire communities as depleted" (2009, 409). Among SDR's many tenets, two of the most important are an identification with the community in opposition to the mainstream and the communicator/designer assuming community ownership without identifying with the inevitability or benevolence of institutions. These two tenets allow researchers to prioritize a community's sovereignty and survival tactics and to establish relationships with communities—relationships that are "mutually beneficial, with an emphasis on the real, positive outcomes for communities in both the short and long term" (Tuck 2009, 424). One specific rhetorical quality of SDR is that the communicator/designer, using personal narratives and narrative detail, privileges, contextualizes, and validates the perspective of constituents. These elements—namely, narrative and identifying with the most affected—have implications for three areas in technical and professional communication, which are discussed in further detail in the following sections related to pedagogy, critical race theory in participatory action research, and expertise in public engagement design.

PEDAGOGY

As a rhetorical heuristic for community engagement, SDR can be applied to technical communication courses, particularly those with community-based or service-based components. The purpose of SDR is to advance the role of the technical communicator from interpreter/translator to technical communicator-as-actant. The former casts the technical communicator as a ghostly figure or as a mere participant in institutional processes. The latter casts the technical communicator as an agential figure in a resistance narrative. Some may doubt the potential for resistance among technical communicators who often perform work on behalf of institutions. This institutionality, however, is what provides technical communicators unique insight into communicative conflict, since they are typically responsible for articulating multiple audiences and stakeholder interests. My investment in the liminality of the technical writer is informed by a critical race perspective that holds that the multiple consciousnesses of minority subjects offer powerful, actionable awareness of hegemony's contradictions. Spillers (2003), for example, argued that

> The fact of domination is alterable only to the extent that the dominated subject recognizes the potential power of its own "double-consciousness.' The subject is certainly seen, but she also sees. It is this return of the gaze that negotiates at every point a space for living, and it is the latter that we must willingly name the counter-power, the counter-mythology. (163)

SDR can help technical communicators and technical communication students instantiate a rhetorical double-consciousness as they place themselves in a counternarrative to their own institutionality.

As described in the previous chapter, SDR has three pillars—definition, ethos, and rhetoric—each of which can be configured into course activities and lesson plans. The first SDR pillar—definition—simply defines sovereignty as the networks, behaviors, forms of knowledge, and ways of life that community members have developed despite, irrespective of, or in response to institutionalism. This definition is useful for outlining what sovereignty might look like, but it purposely does not provide specifics, as sovereign practices differ among communities. Thus, a foundational classroom activity would be asking students to define sovereignty according to a community as they engage in community work. For example, in a business writing course I taught, students completed an assignment wherein they wrote a proposal for planting more trees in an urban area. In a scenario where SDR is practiced, students would work with community members to identify what problem more trees would solve. Methods used in this case might be interviews, ethnography, or discourse analysis. The key here is that, in SDR, students' methods must be justified as being practiced and understood by the community in question. This is in line with the SDR principle of demystifying methods. Once the problem is identified using communally mediated methods, students could then use those same methods (or potentially other methods like storyboarding, collages, or modeling) to research and document how their respective community is already addressing the problem identified. Lastly, students would use the established methods as well as their own rhetorical skills to represent the ways in which community-based problem-solving runs counter to institutional, preconceived notions about a community's problems.

This three-part process—identify, document, counter—could be repeated in the other two pillars: ethos and rhetoric. Ethos refers to a technical communicator/student's rhetorical positioning. This second pillar does not necessarily require such a methodological emphasis, since this is a less research-intensive stage. Instead, this pillar is more rhetorical-compositional. In fact, because it is rhetorical, it would be practiced at every level of the engagement. Some characteristics of this pillar are that the communicator/student prioritizes lived experience, illustrates historical consciousness, avoids appeals to exceptionalism, and assumes community ownership without identifying with the inevitability or benevolence of institutions. In this regard, a simple self-reflection activity at any point in the engagement may be effective. This self-reflection would be part of the "identify" and "counter" parts of the SDR process and could take the form of an essay, interview, or digital media project in which the student answers questions like, "In what ways do I rhetorically and methodologically prioritize lived experience?"; "How can I illustrate a community's historical consciousness?"; and, "How will I assume community ownership?" The answers to these questions would be the "document" phase of the SDR process. The final pillar—rhetoric—refers to the specific rhetorical strategies that a student uses throughout the design/community engagement. Rhetorically, SDR prioritizes narrative and the perspectives of the affected. For this pillar, a formative rubric could be effective. These assessments, in which students identify, document, and counter, can take the form of discussion groups, self-assessments, journaling, and peer review/workshops (which can include non-academic community members in addition to other students).

With some of the methodological tools I've mentioned, SDR contains some elements of participatory design and participatory action research. SDR, however, resists the participatory capture prevalent in HOPE VI. Specifically, SDR does not recruit participants—it functions as its own critical-rhetorical methodology wherein researchers, designers, and students perform community work with community members. Moreover, with the crucial first pillar of "definition," students and researchers do the work of making visible the seemingly invisible by highlighting the work that community members already do to solve their own problems, in a counternarrative to hegemonic rhetoric. These counternarratives act as a check against institutionalism and capture. Another check on capture is SDR's built-in reflexivity, which asks students and community members to evaluate the ethical and rhetorical character of the engagement. SDR's application in a community-based course would require significant cooperation with community members. This cooperation, however, is critical for ensuring an ethical engagement; for helping students, instructors, and others to think through their social and ontological positioning; and for significant student development in research, technical communication, and rhetorical effectiveness. With those advantages in mind, SDR has multiple applications. The next section examines SDR's potential in one research domain in particular—participatory action research.

CRITICAL RACE THEORY IN PARTICIPATORY ACTION RESEARCH

Critical race theory (CRT) has taken up participatory action research (PAR) as an effective method for confronting oppression with and on behalf of vulnerable stakeholders. Within this framework, CRT scholars like Dixson et al. (2018) attempt "to center, privilege, and affirm the voices and perspectives of the communities within which they work" (2018, 65). Importantly, SDR strengthens the application of this theoretical-methodological marriage between CRT and PAR in two key aspects. First, SDR can help technical communicators assume a sovereign ethos, which I defined as the rhetorical positioning of designers, communicators, and audiences as they practice or signify sovereignty. The help comes in identifying the markers of participatory engagement that works against sovereignty. These markers, as exemplified in the neoliberal legitimation strategies that characterized HOPE VI, have been elaborated in previous chapters.

Secondly, SDR's rhetorical topoi can assist technical communicators in implementing textual/communicative strategies that emphasize narrative and identification with the oppressed. While SDR can be taken up by any communicator/designer, the rhetorical framework should lead practitioners to question and think through the ways that they may or may not identify with the groups or cultures involved in the design project. For instance, CRT-based researchers are "committed to social improvement as determined by marginalized and oppressed groups, particularly along lines of race, socio-economic status, and gender" (Dixson et al. 2018, 65). Crucially, "PAR aims to disrupt the dichotomy routinely constructed between researcher and participant" (Dixson et al. 2018, 65). Here, there exists some methodological overlap between SDR and PAR because PAR "values the knowledge of participants as a starting point in the investigation to bring about social change and to challenge institutions of power in addressing social justice issues" (Dixson et al. 2018, 70). Both SDR and PAR enact the perspective that "participants" have knowledge and practices that can bring about social change but that which are also undermined by capture and hegemonic institutionalism. The differences between the two are that PAR is not a rhetorical approach nor is it an inherent design framework. SDR is a rhetorical framework applied in design, participatory, and public engagements and, in that way, can function as a meta-methodological approach.

It is important to emphasize that, certainly from a critical race perspective, sovereignty does not inherently refer to land claims or linguistic group membership. Instead, sovereignty signifies the validity of the knowledge and ways of being that sustain a shared culture, often in resistance to national and international exercises of socioeconomic, police, and military violence. Sovereignty means less the ability to dictate geospatial boundaries and more the resilience of common identification—an identification not only by geospatial organization but also by confronting the institutional power that mobilizes geospatial organization for hegemonic purposes. For instance, Cahill (2010) argues for PAR as a way of reframing issues of immigration. She writes,

> Erasing the global context, the dominant metanarrative identifies "'immigration" itself as the problem. The language within this framework reflects a privileged standpoint and is anything but neutral. Illegal aliens, border security, citizenship, criminals and guest temporary workers are branded as part of the problem that must be addressed. (Cahill 2010, 152–153)

Moreover, a reframing of immigration "represents ontological and epistemological shifts, new ways of knowing and being in the world, informed by the stories of young immigrants' negotiations of the contradictions of everyday life" (Cahill 153). SDR aspires to the reframing mentioned by Cahill, and the ontological considerations that accompany SDR's critical perspective are crucial rhetorical steps toward enacting a reframing. Consequently, rhetorical, ontological, and epistemological shifts force technical communicators to reconsider the role of expertise in participatory and public work.

PUBLIC POLICY: EXPERTISE IN PUBLIC ENGAGEMENT DESIGN

Expertise is signified within the general social domain of knowledge and how knowledge is represented discursively (i.e., literacy, credentials, titles, dress, etc.). In other words, people generally know who an expert is based upon (1) the way the expert talks, (2) if the expert conforms to what an expert in a particular field should look like, and (3) whether the expert has been validated or approved by an institution. At the same time, however, expertise manifests in the power an expert wields in determining outcomes. Accordingly, the distinction between expert/non-expert is not inherently static. Moreover, what counts as "expertise" is not fixed. HOPE VI's participatory framework suggests, however, that expertise is not deployed solely at the level of knowledge; rather, expertise is deployed at the level of power. The power laden within expertise complicates efforts in technical communication to improve public engagement methods and community work. Specifically, the persistence of inequity casts some doubt on the efficacy of deliberative democracy, which structures typical notions of public engagement and dialogue. While SDR (and PAR) accept uneven power relations as given, public engagement frameworks take them as evidentiary; meaning that, while SDR works from a proven, endemic harm, participatory and public engagements often rely on deliberative-democratic frameworks wherein institutional harms are investigated, parsed, and validated by multiple stakeholders. The problem with the latter approach is that it tends to rhetorically and programmatically put controversies on equal footing in a domain evocative of positivism. One such deliberative approach that has tried to move past these shortcomings is hybrid forums.

Hybrid forums are open meetings and public forums between technical experts and "lay people" wherein they publicly discuss controversial topics that affect multiple stakeholders. Generally organized by experts and institutional representatives, these forums are created to highlight the voices of the affected and the marginalized within broader decision-making discussions. Additional goals are for experts to learn more about unanticipated problems and for stakeholders to come to an agreement on solutions. Amilien et al. (2019) indicate that "the objective of hybrid forums is to propose a dialogue, create awareness, facilitate collective exploration and learning, cooperation and integration of a plurality of points of view—on a given controversy" (2019, 3152). This objective leads me to pose several secondary questions: Hybrid forums propose dialogue by and among whom? Whose awareness is being created? Given certain controversies, who or what determines the value of a plurality of which points of view?

While hybrid forums are meant to host these questions rather than to answer them, a potential shortcoming in hybrid forums (as with many public deliberative contexts) is that there is no substantial accounting for the ways in which power, expertise, and rhetorical positioning affect the answers to the questions posed above. With SDR, deliberative communicators/designers can promote a more controversial, critical approach against the institutional power subsuming many public engagement projects. Amilien et al. recognized the issues with hybrid forums and proposed hybrid forums 2.0 or HF 2.0, writing that "The attractiveness of HF 2.0. comprises their practical use (as communication tool), their theoretical perspective (dialogic discussion not aiming to make compromises by mutual discovering, learning and co-constructing knowledge), and methodological application (data gathering)" (2019, 3157). Conversely, SDR would highlight that practicality is not a universal or even a mutual standard and that knowledge is already co-constructed, since the affected and hegemonic institutions rely on each other for their ontological positioning. Moreover, HF 2.0 appears to appropriate some of the neoliberal institutional language that marked HOPE VI, when Amilien et al. write, "An HF 2.0. approach offers to map human resources within a local community to address specific controversies and identify the mechanisms and drivers that can stimulate innovations and co-construct knowledge together" (3157). The appeals to "resources" and "innovations" evoke the community building practiced by HOPE VI, in which participants were programmatically functionalized and rhetorically undermined for institutional purposes.

The problem of participatory capture is an ontological problem in addition to a rhetorical one, and it poses a persistent barrier to deliberation-based engagement, and thus to public policy, because not every voice carries the same degree of power in a forum. Teston et al. (2014) had previously recognized this ontological problem, writing, "eligibility for . . . participation at forums . . . should be decided upon participants' experiences based in practices. . . . This means that we must shift our notion of expertise, or at least the grounds upon which expertise is legitimated, away from an anecdote/data divide and toward ontological multiplicity" (Teston et al. 2014, 166). A lack of ontological identification with the affected risks the perpetuation of a hegemonic gaze and the suppression of sovereignty. This suppression may very well manifest in HF 2.0's second procedural step, "the set-up of the hybrid forum." This step "consists of a preparatory workshop which aims at reaching a common level of knowledge, accrued via shared information on the subject, brief outline of the HF 2.0 structure, and awareness about each other's ideas and perspectives" (Amilien et al. 2019, 3158). Step Two is divided into two parts, where

> part one is limited to the organizing research team, invited panelists (a group of local stakeholders, including entrepreneurs and consumers), and two invited scientific experts, who ought to deliver a short presentation aimed at stimulating, or even provoking, the panelists, by putting forward original ideas or new information. (Amilien et al. 2019, 3158–3159)

Meanwhile, "part two . . . consists of an open public dialogue of about one hour, with a much larger audience, where everybody can contribute to the discussion" (Amilien et al. 2019, 3159). While HF 2.0 seems like an effective deliberative process for coordinating multiple stakeholders, HOPE VI has taught us that merely coordinating or hosting myriad stakeholders is not inherently beneficial to anyone other than those carrying out the coordination. Additionally, though the hybrid forum seeks to account for the voices of the marginalized, the forum flattens or tokenizes the social and rhetorical methods that the marginalized have practiced in resisting (as opposed to finding common ground with) institutions. Thus, SDR has the potential to augment public engagement methods by centralizing the lived experiences of the affected and by avoiding suppressive gestures toward equality.

These suppressive gestures necessitate a reimagination of hybrid forums; after all, "inclusion is not enough" and hybrid forums should account for stakeholders' ontological positioning and "enact not only heterogeneous stakeholder inclusion but also allow for what we re-read as the ontologies that stakeholders bring to bear upon the deliberation" (Teston et al. 2014, 150, 165). In this way, hybrid forums should "encourage the participants to talk about truth and knowledge in ways that are operationalized by the underlying ontology" (Teston et al. 2014, 160). SDR helps designers/communicators to take up these ontological issues from a rhetorical standpoint by outlining a sovereign ethos that prioritizes lived experience, illustrates historical consciousness, demystifies methods, acknowledges structural oppositions, makes visible the seemingly invisible, and ascribes value to internalized difference. In contrast,

> hybridity is not achieved . . . when eligibility for full participation as a party is based on expert "knowledge." Indeed, such an epistemological orientation will unavoidably marginalize anyone outside the . . . mainstream as members of the outside "laity." This sort of perspectivalism is exactly what the ontological approach seeks to avoid. (Teston et al. 2014, 166)

HOPE VI's participatory capture, however, suggests that the ontology of participation lends itself to entrenched marginalization—a marginalization brought about by perspectivalism, not just in knowledge but also in the institutional power that "knowledge" and "expertise" mobilize.

DIRECTIONS FOR FUTURE RESEARCH

Participatory capture asserts power over the marginalized, albeit in often subtle ways whereby institutions mobilize expertise by delimiting outcomes and possibilities in a given domain. In mixed-income/public housing development, residents are rhetorically positioned to participate in a predetermined result, closing off confrontation and strengthening the institution. Recently, McCormack Baron Companies illustrated the fungibility of participatory rhetorics by including resident spotlights on its LinkedIn profile. McCormack is the nation's premier mixed-income development firm, responsible for dozens of HOPE VI and Choice Neighborhood projects. While, with resident voices and narratives, resident spotlights demonstrated potential ways toward a sovereign rhetoric, the framework of inclusion serves to undermine sovereignty. By iterating the power of institutions to use participants' likenesses (i.e., the ontological positioning of the participant), resident spotlights beg the question that those who can manipulate gaze are rarely the ones being scrutinized. For example, McCormack uses the same strategy in its LinkedIn posts as the HOPE VI literature did, which entailed including an image of a smiling Black woman, while using the language of rehabilitation and progress. One McCormack LinkedIn post deploys the legitimation strategy of contrasting the old and the new, evoking the bio/necropolitical intervention that makes the old new and the decaying revitalized (McCormack Baron Companies 2021b).

This rhetorical criticism is an indictment neither on the quality of the McCormack building nor on the quality of life for some of the residents post development. Rather, the rhetorical criticism is based on the ways in which institutions (in this case, McCormack) foreclose and preclude possibilities for dissensus by asserting their institutionality over the rhetorical and ontological position of the most vulnerable participants. In another instance of this institutional assertion, another LinkedIn post from McCormack "welcomes" residents back to Beecher Terrace, a housing project in Louisville's Russell development. That residents were displaced and provided the stipulated privilege of returning to their communities reflects the legal, social, and material divestiture that afflicts many vulnerable residents and conditions the persistent inequities of participation. The same post contains a quote from a Black woman (who is also pictured performing labor on the development worksite), in which the resident seems to privilege sovereignty, or the lived experiences that sustain her and her community. "I miss living at Beecher," she says. "I hope when I move back in that me and my kids have our own space" (McCormack Baron Companies 2021a).

The inclusion of resident voice, however, is merely that—an inclusion. Regarding hybrid forums, for instance, inclusion is not an efficacious mode of controversy or contest. Instead, inclusion (i.e., participation) is an institutional mode of rhetorical management that fails to account for the ontological re-positioning that SDR seeks to offer. Namely, with its resident spotlights, McCormack still communicates from the position of its institutionality. SDR, on the other hand, encourages communicators to speak, write, and design from the position of the affected. For institutions, this can be a challenge, since powerful institutions are rarely made up of the affected or the most vulnerable. McCormack seems to recognize this challenge. On Martin Luther King (MLK) Day 2021, the company posted on its website that

> During this unsettling time when COVID-19, political turmoil, and our national shame of racism dominate our attention, it is more important than ever to create connections—and to advocate for and support all people, especially those who have been suppressed and denied access to the same opportunities as others in their communities. ("A Message on MLK Jr. Day" 2021)

In this instance, McCormack seeks to identify with readers by appealing to controversial topics. The company also acknowledges the fact of ontological difference in implying social and material characteristics of distinct lived experiences. However, McCormack also resorts to the same ontological flattening found in appeals to nationalism and inclusion, with phrases like "our national shame" and "all people." Later, in the same post, the company writes, "At McCormack Baron, one of our core values is 'social responsibility—investing our resources to strengthen communities.' This value drives us to see ourselves as participants in the communities in which we work" ("A Message on MLK Jr. Day" 2021). Beyond the rhetorical configuration of certain communities as both "weak" and as investment opportunities, the company also deploys the rhetoric of participatory capture by naming itself as a participant, eliding the accountability and power that developers and their institutional partners wield in determining outcomes.

The participatory capture identified in HOPE VI presents technical communicators with opportunities to continually identify and confront how institutions name, use, and configure participation in ways that undermine ethical practices. Additional research can be done to assess how institutional participatory discourses are deployed in other communicative spaces. My project has examined traditional technical communication documents such as reports, manuals, and newsletters. However, McCormack's LinkedIn posts suggest that digital media present opportunities for other archival and rhetorical research. For example, how might social media and user experience/interface design influence participatory development, from the perspectives of both institutions and participants? What are some of the technical, rhetorical, and ethical implications for digital engagement in development contexts? These are just some potential research questions around communication technology. Similarly, this book examines only a few key instances of housing development and geospatial, economic politics. While the texts I've analyzed are representative of larger discursive and rhetorical activity, they also represent only a few communicative moments. More research can be done to map localized, geographical variances in participatory capture relative to other development projects and how local communities have rhetorically resisted capture. Finally, researchers can further consider the place of participatory discourses in issues of environmentalism, policing, transportation, zoning, and other controversial areas of development politics.

Bibliography

Agboka, Godwin Y. 2013. "Participatory Localization: A Social Justice Approach to Navigating Unenfranchised/Disenfranchised Cultural Sites." *Technical Communication Quarterly* 22(1): 28–49.

———. 2014. "Decolonial Methodologies: Social Justice Perspectives in Intercultural Technical Communication Research." *Journal of Technical Writing and Communication* 44(3): 297–327.

Ahmed, Sarah. 2012. *On Being Included: Racism and Diversity in Institutional Life*. Durham: Duke University Press.

Amilien, Virginie, Barbara Tocco, and Paal Strandbakken. 2019. "At the Heart of Controversies: Hybrid Forums as an Experimental Multi-Actor Tool to Enhance Sustainable Practices in Localized Agro-Food Systems." *British Food Journal* 121(12): 3151–3167.

"Architects' Work to Meet Resident Needs, Enhance Community." 2004. *New Beginnings: An Update on the Clarksdale HOPE VI Revitalization*, Clarksdale HOPE VI Revitalization, July 2004. http://www.lmha1.org/pressroom/docs/4_clarksdale_July2004.pdf.

Axtell, Rick, and Michelle Tooley. 2015. "The Other Side of Hope: Squandering Social Capital in Louisville's HOPE VI." *Journal of Poverty* 19(3): 278–304.

Barlieb, Ethan. 2007. "HOPE VI Revitalization Grants: Weighing the Costs and Benefits, and Considering a Solution in the Context of Liberty City, Miami." *University of Miami Business Law Review* 15(201): 201–224.

Barwashi, Anis S., and Mary Jo Reiff. 2010. *Genre: An Introduction to History, Theory, Research, and Pedagogy*. Anderson: Parlor Press.

"A Better Day Will Soon be Underway." 2004. *New Beginnings: An Update on the Clarksdale HOPE VI Revitalization*, Clarksdale HOPE VI Revitalization, July 2004. http://www.lmha1.org/pressroom/docs/4_clarksdale_July2004.pdf.

Berrey, Ellen. 2015. *The Enigma of Diversity: The Language of Race and the Limits of Racial Justice*. Chicago: The University of Chicago Press.

Bilge, Sirma. 2010. "We've Joined the Table but We're Still on the Menu: Clickbaiting Diversity in Today's University." In *Routledge International Handbook of Contemporary Racisms*, edited by John Solomos, 317–331. London: Routledge.

Björgvinsson, Erling, Pelle Ehn, and Per-Anders Hillgren. 2012. "Agonistic Participatory Design: Working with Marginalised Social Movements." *CoDesign* 8(2–3): 127–144.

Blyler, Nancy. 1998. "'Taking a Political Turn': The Critical Perspective and Research in Technical Communication." *Technical Communication Quarterly* 7(1): 33–52.

Britt, Elizabeth C. 2006. "The Rhetorical Work of Institutions." In *Critical Power Tools: Technical Communication and Cultural Studies*, edited by J Blake Scott, Bernadette Longo, and Katherine V. Wills, 133–150. Albany: SUNY Press.

"Building a New Life." 2004. *New Beginnings: An Update on the Clarksdale HOPE VI Revitalization*, Clarksdale HOPE VI Revitalization, July 2004. http://www.lmha1.org/pressroom/docs/4_clarksdale_July2004.pdf.

Cahill, Caitlin. 2010. "'Why Do *They* Hate *Us*?' Reframing Immigration through Participatory Action Research." *Area* 42(2):152–161.

Cameron, Ed. 2020. "'Whence Comes This Uncanniest of All Guests?' Extimate Nihilism in the Horror Films of Jordan Peele." *Literature/Film Quarterly* 48(3). https://www.jstor.org/stable/48678476.

Center on Budget and Policy Priorities. 2024. "A Blueprint for Prosperity: Expanding Housing Affordability: Testimony of Peggy Bailey, Vice President for Housing and Income Security, Center on Budget and Policy Priorities, Before the Senate Budget Committee." January 31, 2024. https://www.cbpp.org/research/housing/a-blueprint-for-prosperity-expanding-housing-affordability#_edn15.

Chakravartty, Paula, and Denise Ferreira da Silva. 2012. "Accumulation, Dispossession, and Debt: The Racial Logic of Global Capitalism—An Introduction." *American Quarterly* 64(3): 361–385.

Chenault, Tiffany Gayle. 2015. *The Unseen Politics of Public Housing: Resident Councils, Communities, and Change.* Lanham, Maryland: Lexington Books.

City of Columbus. 2003. *The South Linden Neighborhood Plan.* Department of Development, Planning Division. Columbus, Ohio, December 2003. https://issuu.com/ourlinden/docs/south-linden-plan_2003.

———. 2012. *The South Linden Neighborhood Plan Amendment.* Department of Development, Planning Division. Columbus, Ohio, November 2012. https://www.columbus.gov/WorkArea/DownloadAsset.aspx?id=2147489249.

"Clarksdale HOPE VI Initiative Underway." 2005. *New Beginnings: An Update on the Clarksdale HOPE VI Revitalization,* Clarksdale HOPE VI Revitalization, First Quarter 2005. http://www.lmha1.org/pressroom/docs/1stquart_2005__Newsletter.pdf.

"Clarksdale Resident Council Takes Office." 2003. *New Beginnings: An Update on the Clarksdale HOPE VI Revitalization,* Clarksdale HOPE VI Revitalization, July 2003. http://www.lmha1.org/pressroom/docs/3_clarks_july_2003_newsletter.pdf.

"Clarksdale Resident Interviews Underway." 2003. *New Beginnings: An Update on the Clarksdale HOPE VI Revitalization,* Clarksdale HOPE VI Revitalization, July 2003. http://www.lmha1.org/pressroom/docs/3_clarks_july_2003_newsletter.pdf.

Cleaver, Frances. 1999. "Paradoxes of Participation: Questioning Participatory Approaches to Development." *Journal of International Development* 11(4): 597–612.

"Community and Supportive Services (CSS)." 2005. *New Beginnings: An Update on the Clarksdale HOPE VI Revitalization,* Clarksdale HOPE VI Revitalization, First Quarter 2005. http://www.lmha1.org/pressroom/docs/1stquart_2005__Newsletter.pdf.

Conte, Julia, and Janet Li. 2013. "Neoliberal Urban Revitalization in Chicago." *Advocates' Forum*: 19–30.

Cook, Joan. 1975. "Fresh Federal Aid and Tenant Gains Bring a New Era for Jersey Project." *New York Times*, July 28, 1975. https://www.nytimes.com/1975/07/28/archives/fresh-federal-aid-and-tenant-gains-bring-a-new-era-for-jersey.html.

"Cuomo Announces $35 Million HOPE VI Grant to Atlanta to Transform Public Housing and Help Residents." 1999. U.S. Department of Housing and Urban Development Archives, August 14, 1999. https://archives.hud.gov/news/1999/pr99-157.html.

Day, Iyko. 2015. "Being or Nothingness: Indigeneity, Antiblackness, and Settler Colonial Critique." *Critical Ethnic Studies* 1(2):102–121.

Demsas, Jerusalem. 2022. "Community Input Is Bad, Actually." *The Atlantic*, April 22, 2022. https://www.theatlantic.com/ideas/archive/2022/04/local-government-community-input-housing-public-transportation/629625/.

"Diversity Marketing." 2020. Marketing Schools, November 17, 2020. https://www.marketing-schools.org/types-of-marketing/diversity-marketing/.

Dixson, Adrienne D., ArCasia James, and Brittany L. Frieson. 2019. "Taking It to the Streets: Critical Race Theory, Participatory Research and Social Justice." In *Understanding Critical Race Research Methods and Methodologies*, edited by Jessica T. DeCuir-Gunby, Thandeka K. Chapman, and Paul A. Schutz, 64–75. 1st ed. London: Routledge.

Dore, Mayane. 2023. "Governing through Design: The Politics of Participation in Neoliberal Cities." *CoDesign* 19(3): 253–268.

"Dreaming Big and Doing Things Right." 2003. *New Beginnings: An Update on the Clarksdale HOPE VI Revitalization,* Clarksdale HOPE VI Revitalization, July 2003. http://www.lmha1.org/pressroom/docs/3_clarks_july_2003_newsletter.pdf.

"Dreams from a New Community." 2004. *New Beginnings: An Update on the Clarksdale HOPE VI Revitalization,* Clarksdale HOPE VI Revitalization, July 2004. http://www.lmha1.org/pressroom/docs/4_clarksdale_July2004.pdf.

Duryea, Danielle Pelfrey. 2006. "Gendering the Gentrification of Public Housing: HOPE VI's Disparate Impact on Lowest-Income African American Women." *Georgetown Journal on Poverty Law and Policy* 13(3): 567–593.

"DuValle Education Center, Real Hope Brings Real Changes." 2003. *The View: The Villages at Park DuValle,* the Community Builders, Inc., June/July 2003, Vol. 3, Issue 3. http://www.lmha1.org/pressroom/docs/1_pd_july_2003newsletter.pdf.

Evia, Carlos, and Ashley Patriarca. 2012. "Beyond Compliance: Participatory Translation of Safety Communication for Latino Construction Workers." *Journal of Business and Technical Communication* 26(3): 340–367.

Fairclough, Norman. 2012. "Critical Discourse Analysis." In *The Routledge Handbook of Discourse Analysis*, edited by Michael Handford and James Paul Gee, 9–20. London: Routledge.

"Father Daughter Dance." 2016. *Russell Choice Neighborhood Planning Initiative*, Louisville Metro Housing Authority, March 2016. http://www.lmha1.org/March%202016%20Newsletter.pdf.

Fleming, David. 2008. *City of Rhetoric: Revitalizing the Public Sphere in Metropolitan America*. Albany: SUNY Press.

Foss, Sonja. K. 2018. *Rhetorical Criticism: Exploration and Practice*. 5th ed. Long Grove, IL: Waveland Press, Inc.

Foucault, Michel. 2007. *Security, Territory, Population: Lectures at the Collège de France, 1977–1978*. New York: Picador.

"4th District Reports Crime Is Down." 2003. *The View: The Villages at Park DuValle*, the Community Builders, Inc., June/July 2003 Vol. 3, Issue 3. http://www.lmha1.org/pressroom/docs/1_pd_july_2003newsletter.pdf.

Gilderbloom John, Brazley Michael D., and Pan Zhenfeng. 2005. "HOPE VI: A Study of Housing and Neighborhood Satisfaction." *Sustain: A Journal of Environmental and Sustainability* 11: 1–26.

Goldberg, David Theo. 2009. *The Threat of Race: Reflections on Racial Neoliberalism*. Chicester: Wiley-Blackwell.

Gonzales, Teresa Irene. 2021. *Building a Better Chicago: Race and Community Resistance to Urban Redevelopment*. New York: New York University Press.

Grant, David, Cynthia Hardy, Cliff Oswick, and Linda Putnam. 2004. "Introduction: Organizational Discourse: Exploring the Field." In *The SAGE Handbook of Organizational Discourse*, edited by David Grant, Cynthia Hardy, Cliff Oswick and Linda L. Putnam, 1–36. London: Sage Publications.

Greenbaum, Susan D. 2015. *Blaming the Poor: The Long Shadow of the Moynihan Report on Cruel Images about Poverty*. New Brunswick, NJ: Rutgers University Press.

Greene, Matthew H. 2008. "The Hope VI Paradox: Why Do HUD's Most Successful Housing Developments Fail to Benefit the Poorest of the Poor?" *Journal of Law and Policy* 17(1): 191–229.

Gronouwe, Lucas, Matthijs Moorkamp, and Max Visser. 2021. "Towards Emancipation through Organizational (Re)design? Exploring Integral Organizational Renewal from a Critical Management Perspective." *International Journal of Organizational Analysis* 30(7): 34–48.

Haas, Angela M. 2012. "Race, Rhetoric, and Technology: A Case Study of Decolonial Technical Communication Theory, Methodology, and Pedagogy." *Journal of Business and Technical Communication* 26(3): 277–310.

Haas, Angela M., and Michelle F. Eble. 2018. "Introduction." In *Key Theoretical Frameworks: Teaching Technical Communication in the Twenty-First Century*, edited by edited by Angela M. Haas and Michelle F. Eble, 1–19. Utah: Utah State University Press.

Handley, Derek. G. 2019. "'The Line Drawn': Freedom Corner and Rhetorics of Place in Pittsburgh, 1960s-2000s." *Rhetoric Review* 38(2): 173–189.

Hanifa, Raheem. 2022. "This Year, Half as Many Black Households Can Afford a Home as Last Year." Harvard Joint Center for Housing Studies, August 17, 2022. https://www.jchs.harvard.edu/blog/year-half-many-black-households-can-afford-home-last-year.

Hartman, Saidiya V. 1997. *Scenes of Subjection: Terror, Slavery, and Self-Making in Nineteenth-Century America.* New York: Oxford University Press.

"Have You Met the Russell Neighborhood Outreach Workers?" 2015. *Russell Choice Neighborhood Planning Initiative,* Louisville Metro Housing Authority, September 2015. http://www.lmha1.org/Russell_Newsletter_event_edits.pdf.

Herndl, Carl G. 1993. "Teaching Discourse and Reproducing Culture: A Critique of Professional and Nonacademic Writing." *College Composition and Communication* 44: 349–363.

Herrmann, Thomas, and Thomas Walter. 1997. "Participatory Design and Cyclic Improvement of Business Processes with Workflow Management Systems." Proc. of Americas Conference on Information Systems (AIS).

"Home Depot Comes to Park DuValle." 2004. *The View: The Villages at Park DuValle*, the Community Builders, Inc., Jan/Feb 2004 Vol. 3, Issue 3. http://www.lmha1.org/pressroom/docs/2_pd_jan_2004Newsletter.pdf.

"Home for the Holidays in Park DuValle." 2004. *The View: The Villages at Park DuValle*, the Community Builders, Inc., Jan/Feb 2004 Vol. 3, Issue 3. http://www.lmha1.org/pressroom/docs/2_pd_jan_2004Newsletter.pdf.

"Honoring a Model Community and Those Who Are Models for Our Children." 2003. *The View: The Villages at Park DuValle,* the Community Builders, Inc., June/July 2003, Vol. 3, Issue 3. http://www.lmha1.org/pressroom/docs/1_pd_july_2003newsletter.pdf.

Howcroft, Debra, and Melanie Wilson. 2003. "Paradoxes of Participatory Practices: The Janus Role of the Systems Developer." *Information and Organization* 13(1): 1–24.

"HUD Officials Meet with Residents—Review Process, Encourages Involvement." 2003. *New Beginnings: An Update on the Clarksdale HOPE VI Revitalization,* Clarksdale HOPE VI Revitalization, July 2003. http://www.lmha1.org/pressroom/docs/3_clarks_july_2003_newsletter.pdf.

Hyra, Derek S. 2012. "Conceptualizing the New Urban Renewal: Comparing the Past to the Present." *Urban Affairs Review* 48(4): 498–527.

"Intergenerational Computer Program a Hit." 2005. *The View: The Villages at Park DuValle*, the Community Builders, Inc., March 2005, Vol. 4, Issue 1. http://www.lmha1.org/pressroom/docs/parkduvalle_news_march05.pdf.

"Introducing the Choice Neighborhoods Planning Initiative: Vision Russell." 2015. *Russell Choice Neighborhood Planning Initiative*, Louisville Metro Housing Authority, September 2015. http://www.lmha1.org/Russell_Newsletter_event_edits.pdf.

"A Joint Meeting of All CNI Task Forces." 2016. *Russell Choice Neighborhood Planning Initiative*, Louisville Metro Housing Authority, April 2016. http://www.lmha1.org/April%202016%20Newsletter.pdf.

Jones, Katherine T., and Jeff Popke. 2010. "Re-Envisioning the City: Lefebvre, HOPE VI, and the Neoliberalization of Urban Space." *Urban Geography* 31(1): 114–133.

Jones, Natasha N. 2016. "The Technical Communicator as Advocate: Integrating a Social Justice Approach in Technical Communication." *Journal of Technical Writing and Communication* 46(3): 342–361.

Jones, Natasha N., Kristen R. Moore, and Rebecca Walton. 2016. "Disrupting the Past to Disrupt the Future: An Antenarrative of Technical Communication." *Technical Communication Quarterly* 25(4): 211–229.

Jones, Natasha N., and Rebecca Walton. 2018. "Using Narratives to Foster Critical Thinking about Diversity and Social Justice." In *Key Theoretical Frameworks: Teaching Technical Communication in the Twenty-First Century*, edited by Angela M. Haas and Michelle F. Eble, 241–267. Utah: Utah State University Press.

Kaethler, Michael, Seppe De Blust, and Tim Devos. 2017. "Ambiguity as Agency: Critical Opportunists in the Neoliberal City." *CoDesign* 13(3): 175–186.

Kasdan, Alexa, Erin Markman, and Pat Convey. 2014. *A People's Budget: A Research and Evaluation Report on Participatory Budgeting in New York City*. New York: Community Development Project at the Urban Justice Center.

King, Tiffany Lethabo. 2016. "The Labor of (Re)reading Plantation Landscapes Fungible(ly)." *Antipode* 48: 1022–1039.

Kingsley, G Thomas, Joseph B McNeely, and James O Gibson. 1997. *Community Building: Coming of Age*. Policy File. Urban Institute.

Kirszbaum, Thomas. 2019. "Urban Renewal in the USA: A Neoliberal Policy?" *Métropolitiques*, May 3, 2019. https://www.metropolitiques.eu/Urban-Renewal-in-the-USA-A-Neoliberal-Policy.html

Kohl-Arenas, Erica. 2011. "Governing Poverty Amidst Plenty: Participatory Development and Private Philanthropy." *Geography Compass* 5(11): 811–824.

Kost, Thomas C. 2012. "Hope After HOPE VI?: Reaffirming Racial Integration as a Primary Goal in Housing Policy Prescriptions." *Northwestern University Law Review* 106(3): 1379–1418.

Laffont, Jean-Jacques, and Jean Tirole. 1991. "The Politics of Government Decision-Making: A Theory of Regulatory Capture." *The Quarterly Journal of Economics* 106(4): 1089–1127.

Lang, Marion. 2023. "Discreet Empowerment: Race- and Gender-separated Participatory Mechanisms in French Working-class Neighbourhoods." *European Journal of Cultural and Political Sociology* 10(1): 98–126.

Larsen, Anne Karin, Vishanthie Sewpaul, and Grete Oline Hole. 2014. "Introduction." In *Participation in Community Work: International Perspectives*, edited by Anne Karin Larsen, Vishanthie Sewpaul, and Grete Oline Hole, 1–15. London: Routledge.

Lee, Caroline W. 2015. "Participatory Practices in Organizations." *Sociology Compass* 9(4): 272–288.

Lenette, Caroline. 2022. *Participatory Action Research: Ethics and Decolonization*. New York: Oxford University Press.

Lerner, Josh, and Donata Secondo. 2012. "By the People, For the People: Participatory Budgeting from the Bottom up in North America." *Journal of Public Deliberation* 8(2): 1–9.

Longo, Bernadette. 2006. "An Approach for Applying Cultural Study Theory to Technical Writing Research." In *Critical Power Tools: Technical Communication and Cultural Studies*, edited by J. Blake Scott, Katherine V. Wills, and Bernadette Longo, 111–131. Albany: SUNY Press.

"Louisville: A National Leader in Revitalization." 2005. *New Beginnings: An Update on the Clarksdale HOPE VI Revitalization*, Clarksdale HOPE VI Revitalization, First Quarter 2005. http://www.lmha1.org/pressroom/docs/1stquart_2005__Newsletter.pdf.

"Louisville Receives HOPE VI Grant—Revitalization to Provide Range of Opportunities." 2003. *New Beginnings: An Update on the Clarksdale HOPE VI Revitalization*, Clarksdale HOPE VI Revitalization, July 2003. http://www.lmha1.org/pressroom/docs/3_clarks_july_2003_newsletter.pdf.

Lund, Jens Friis, and Moeko Saito-Jensen. 2013. "Revisiting the Issue of Elite Capture of Participatory Initiatives." *World Development* 46: 104–112.

Lyons, Scott Richard. 2000. "Rhetorical Sovereignty: What Do American Indians Want from Writing?" *College Composition and Communication* 51(3): 447–468.

"Making It Happen Communication Central." 2003. *New Beginnings: An Update on the Clarksdale HOPE VI Revitalization*, Clarksdale HOPE VI Revitalization, July 2003. http://www.lmha1.org/pressroom/docs/3_clarks_july_2003_newsletter.pdf.

"Making Way for a New Day." 2005. *New Beginnings: An Update on the Clarksdale HOPE VI Revitalization*, Clarksdale HOPE VI Revitalization, First Quarter 2005. http://www.lmha1.org/pressroom/docs/1stquart_2005__Newsletter.pdf.

Malinconico, Joe. 2021. "Residents Wonder about the Fate of Seth Boyden." *Patch*, July 14, 2011. https://patch.com/new-jersey/newarknj/residents-wonder-about-the-future-of-seth-boyden.

Mayorga, Sarah Ann. 2012. *Preserving the White Picket Fence: Interracial Conduct in an Integrated Neighborhood*. Dissertation, Duke University. https://hdl.handle.net/10161/5553.

Mbembé, Achille, and Libby Meintjes. 2003. "Necropolitics." *Public Culture* 15(1): 11–40.

McCormack Baron Companies. 2021a. "As We Begin Welcoming Residents Back to Beecher Terrace in Louisville, KY, We Would Like to Introduce You to People Who Have Worked on the Project . . ." *LinkedIn*. https://www.linkedin.com/posts/mccormack-baron-companies_peopleofbeecher-beecherterracestories-activity-6770750388992819200-zmPk/.

———. 2021b. "Want to Meet Some of the Residents at the New Beecher Terrace Senior Residence? Meet Valarie Morris, a Former Resident of the 'Old' Beecher Terrace Who Was the 2nd Person to Move into the New Senior Building." *LinkedIn*. https://www.linkedin.com/posts/mccormack-baron-companies_want-to-meet-some-of-the-residents-at-the-activity-6777288487533121536-vLAo/.

McFarlane, Julian, Soroya, Aurora Occa, Wei Peng, Oluwatumininu Awonuga, and Susan E. Morgan. 2022. "Community-Based Participatory Research (CBPR) to Enhance Participation of Racial/Ethnic Minorities in Clinical Trials: A 10-Year Systematic Review." *Health Communication* 37(9): 1075–1092.

McKnight, John L., and John P. Kretzmann. 1990. *Program on Community Development: Mapping Community Capacity*. Center for Urban Affairs and Policy Research.

Merriam-Webster. (n.d.). "Theodicy." In *Merriam-Webster.com dictionary*. https://www.merriam-webster.com/dictionary/theodicy.

"A Message from Metro Councilman Willie Bright, District 4." 2003. *New Beginnings: An Update on the Clarksdale HOPE VI Revitalization*, Clarksdale HOPE VI Revitalization, July 2003. http://www.lmha1.org/pressroom/docs/3_clarks_july_2003_newsletter.pdf.

"A Message on MLK Jr. Day to the McCormack Baron Community." 2021. McCormack Baron Salazar, January 18, 2021. https://www.mccormackbaron.com/news/2021/01/18/a-message-on-mlk-jr.-day-to-the-mccormack-baron-community/.

Middleton, Michael K., Samantha Senda-Cook, and Danielle Endres. 2011. "Articulating Rhetorical Field Methods: Challenges and Tensions." *Western Journal of Communication* 75(4): 386–406.

Miller, David. 2017. "How a Former NBA Player Turned $350,000 into $400 Million." *Black Wealth Channel*, July 28, 2017. https://www.themaven.net/blackwealthchannel/investing/how-a-former-nba-player-turned-350-000-into-400-million-FyRtXUpz5E6XFmVi6NhedA/.

Mohan, Giles, and Kristian Stokke. 2000. "Participatory Development and Empowerment: The Dangers of Localism." *Third World Quarterly* 21(2): 247–268.

Moore, Kristen. R. 2018. "Black Feminist Epistemology as a Framework for Community-based Teaching." In *Key Theoretical Frameworks: Teaching Technical Communication in the Twenty-first Century*, edited by edited by Angela M. Haas and Michelle F. Eble, 185–211. University Press of Colorado.

Moore, Kristen R., and Timothy J. Elliott. 2016. "From Participatory Design to a Listening Infrastructure: A Case of Urban Planning and Participation." *Journal of Business and Technical Communication* 30(1): 59–84.

"Moving Forward." 2004. *The View: The Villages at Park DuValle*, the Community Builders, Inc., Jan/Feb 2004 Vol. 3, Issue 3. http://www.lmha1.org/pressroom/docs/2_pd_jan_2004Newsletter.pdf.

Nash, Jennifer C. 2019. *Black Feminism Reimagined: After Intersectionality*. Durham: Duke University Press.

National Housing Law Project. 2002. *False HOPE: A Critical Assessment of the HOPE VI Public Housing Redevelopment Program.*

Ndubuizu, Rosemary. 2023. "Gendering the Politics of Black Displacement." *Women's Studies Quarterly* 51(1–2): 169–180.

"Neighborhood Survey Completed!" 2015. *Russell Choice Neighborhood Planning Initiative*, Louisville Metro Housing Authority, November 2015. http://www.lmha1.org/November_Newsletter_2015_final_copy.pdf.

"1999 HOPE VI Application: Stella Wright Homes in Newark." 1999. *Abt Associates*. https://www.abtassociates.com/projects/1999-hope-vi-application-stella-wright-homes-in-newark.

Northover, Patricia. 2012. "Abject Blackness, Hauntologies of Development, and the Demand for Authenticity: A Critique of Sen's Development as Freedom." *The Global South* 6(1): 66–86.

Ornatowkski, Cezar M., and Linn K. Bekins. 2004. "What's Civic about Technical Communication? Technical Communication and the Rhetoric of 'Community.'" *Technical Communication Quarterly* 13(3): 251–269.

"Park DuValle Association Organized to Guide Community's Future." 2003. *The View: The Villages at Park DuValle*, the Community Builders, Inc., June/July 2003 Vol. 3, Issue 3. http://www.lmha1.org/pressroom/docs/1_pd_july_2003newsletter.pdf.

"Park DuValle Youth Selected for IDA Program." 2004. *The View: The Villages at Park DuValle*, the Community Builders, Inc., Jan/Feb 2004 Vol. 3, Issue 3. http://www.lmha1.org/pressroom/docs/2_pd_jan_2004Newsletter.pdf.

"Partnership: The Heart of Our Success." 2003. *New Beginnings: An Update on the Clarksdale HOPE VI Revitalization*, Clarksdale HOPE VI Revitalization, July 2003. http://www.lmha1.org/pressroom/docs/3_clarks_july_2003_newsletter.pdf.

Perrone, Nicolás M. 2017. "Neoliberalism and Economic Sovereignty: Property, Contracts, and Foreign Investment Relations." In *Neoliberal Legality: Understanding the Role of Law in the Neoliberal Projec*t, edited by Honor Brabazon, 43–60. London: Routledge.

Pin, Laura. 2020. "Race, Citizenship and Participation: Interrogating the Racial Dynamics of Participatory Budgeting." *New Political Science* 42(4): 578–594.

Pittman, LaShawnDa, and Deirdre Oakley. 2018. "It Was Love in All the Buildings They Tore Down: How Caregiving Grandmothers Create and Experience a Sense of Community in Chicago Public Housing." *City & Community* 17(2): 461–484.

Plowman, Penelope J. 2016. "Participatory Methodologies for Intersectional Research in Organisations." *Journal of Organizational Ethnography* 5(1): 28–43.

Ponton III, David. 2024. *Houston and the Permanence of Segregation: An Afropessimist Approach to Urban History*. Austin: University of Texas Press.

Popkin, Susan J., Bruce Katz, Mary K. Cunningham, Karen D. Brown, Jeremy Gustafson, and Margery Austin Turner. 2004. *A Decade of HOPE VI: Research Findings and Policy Challenges*. Washington, DC: The Urban Institute and The Brookings Institution.

Porter, James E., Patricia Sullivan, Stuart Blythe, Jeffrey T. Grabill, and Libby Miles. 2000. "Institutional Critique: A Rhetorical Methodology for Change." *College Composition and Communication* 51(4): 610–642.

Puri, S. K., and Sundeep Sahay. 2003. "Institutional Structures and Participation." In *Organizational Information Systems in the Context of Globalization*, edited by Mikko Korpela, Ramiro Montealegre, and Angeliki Poulymenakou, 271–287. Boston: Springer.

Quick, Kathryn S., and Martha S. Feldman. 2011. "Distinguishing Participation and Inclusion." *Journal of Planning Education and Research* 31(3): 272–290.

Raelin, Joseph. A. 2012. "Dialogue and Deliberation as Expressions of Democratic Leadership in Participatory Organizational Change." *Journal of Organizational Change Management* 25(1): 7–23.

Rai, Candice. 2016. *Democracy's Lot: Rhetoric, Publics, and the Places of Invention.* Tuscaloosa: The University of Alabama.

"Resident Assessments Provide Insight." 2004. *New Beginnings: An Update on the Clarksdale HOPE VI Revitalization*, Clarksdale HOPE VI Revitalization, July 2004. http://www.lmha1.org/pressroom/docs/4_clarksdale_July2004.pdf.

"Resident Spotlight: Mechele Turner." 2015. *Russell Choice Neighborhood Planning Initiative*, Louisville Metro Housing Authority, October 2015. http://www.lmha1.org/October_Newsletter_2015_Draft_4.pdf.

"Resident Spotlight: Nannie Bibbs." 2016. *Russell Choice Neighborhood Planning Initiative*, Louisville Metro Housing Authority, May 2016. http://www.lmha1.org/May%202016%20Newsletter.pdf.

Rifkin, Mark. 2024. *The Politics of Kinship: Race, Family, Governance.* Durham: Duke University Press.

Rigg Jonathan. 2016. *Challenging Southeast Asian Development: The Shadows of Success.* London: Routledge.

Rose, Emma J., and Alison Cardinal. 2021. "Purpose and Participation: Heuristics for Planning, Implementing, and Reflecting on Social Justice Work." In *Equipping Technical Communicators for Social Justice Work: Theories, Methodologies, and Pedagogies*, edited by Rebecca Walton and Godwin Y. Agboka, 75–97. Utah: Utah State Universit Press.

"Rosewind." *ProPublica.* https://projects.propublica.org/hud/properties/OH001000105.

Rude, Carolyn D. 2009. "Mapping the Research Question in Technical Communication." *Journal of Business and Technical Communication* 23(2): 174–215.

Saiz, Albert. 2023. "The Global Housing Affordability Crisis: Policy Options and Strategies." *IZA Institute of Labor Economics*, October 2023, Policy Paper 203. https://docs.iza.org/pp203.pdf.

Seifer, Sarena D, Margo Michaels, and Stacy Collins. 2010. "Applying Community-Based Participatory Research Principles and Approaches in Clinical Trials: Forging a New Model for Cancer Clinical Research." *Progress in Community Health Partnerships: Research, Education, and Action* 4(1): 37–46.

"Signs of Progress and Accomplishment." 2005. *The View: The Villages at Park DuValle*, the Community Builders, Inc., March 2005 Vol. 4, Issue 1. http://www.lmha1.org/pressroom/docs/parkduvalle_news_march05.pdf.

Silva, Denise Ferreira da. 2007. *Toward a Global Idea of Race*. Minneapolis: University of Minnesota Press.

———. 2009. "No-Bodies: Law, Raciality and Violence." *Griffith Law Review* 18(2): 212–236.

———. 2015. "Globality." *Critical Ethnic Studies* 1(1): 33–38.

Simonsen Jesper, and Toni Robertson. 2013. "Participatory Design: An Introduction." In *Routledge International Handbook of Participatory Design*, edited by Jesper Simonsen and Toni Robertson, 1–17. London: Routledge.

Slack, Jennifer Daryl, David James Miller, and Jeffrey Doak. 1993. "The Technical Communicator as Author: Meaning, Power, Authority." *Journal of Business and Technical communication* 7(1): 12–36.

Smith, Sara, and Pavithra Vasudevan. 2017. "Race, Biopolitics, and the Future: Introduction to the Special Section." *Environment and Planning D: Society and Space* 35(2): 210–221.

Sparre, Mogens. 2020. "Utilizing Participatory Action Research to Change Perception about Organizational Culture from Knowledge Consumption to Knowledge Creation." *SAGE Open* 10(1): 1–9.

Spillers, Hortense J. 2003. *Black, White, and in Color: Essays on American Literature and Culture*. Chicago: University of Chicago Press.

Spinuzzi, Clay. 2003. *Tracing Genres through Organizations: A Sociocultural Approach to Information Design*. Cambridge, Mass: MIT Press.

"Spotlight On Wendy's." 2005. *The View: The Villages at Park DuValle*, the Community Builders, Inc., March 2005 Vol. 4, Issue 1. http://www.lmha1.org/pressroom/docs/parkduvalle_news_march05.pdf.

Stormer, Nathan. 2019. "The Dark Black Dot: On Antiblackness and Rhetoric." Presented October 5, 2019 at the University of South Carolina Conference on Rhetorical Theory, Columbia, SC.

Tahin, Gabor. 2011. "Rhetorical Heuristics: Probabilistic Strategies in Complex Oratorical Arguments." *Argumentation* 25: 1–21.

Taylor, Keeanga-Yamahtta. 2019. *Race for Profit: How Banks and the Real Estate Industry Undermined Black Homeownership*. Chapel Hill: University of North Carolina Press.

Teston, Christa B., S. Scott Graham, Raquel Baldwinson, Andria Li, and Jessamyn Swift. 2014. "Public Voices in Pharmaceutical Deliberations: Negotiating 'Clinical Benefit' in the FDA's Avastin Hearing." *The Journal of Medical Humanities* 35(2): 149–170.

"Theodicy." *Merriam-Webster.com Dictionary*, Merriam-Webster. https://www.merriam-webster.com/dictionary/theodicy.

Tuck, Eve. 2009. "Suspending Damage: A Letter to Communities." *Harvard Educational Review* 79(3): 409–428.

United States Department of Housing and Urban Development. 1979. *Resident Participation in the Housing Management Process: Participant's Workbook*. Washington, DC: United States Department of Housing and Urban Development.

———. 1988. *A Decent Place to Live: The Report of the National Housing Task Force*. HUD. https://www.huduser.gov/portal/Publications/pdf/HUD-5830.pdf.

———. 1996. "Public Housing Demolition, Site Revitalization, and Replacement Housing Grants (HOPE VI). FY 1998 Revitalization Grant Agreement." https://www.hud.gov/sites/documents/DOC_10003.pdf.

———. 1997. *Community Building in Public Housing: Ties That Bind People and Their Communities*. Washington, DC: United States Department of Housing and Urban Development.

———. 1999. *HOPE VI: Building Communities and Transforming Lives*. HUD. https://www.huduser.gov/portal//Publications/pdf/hope.pdf.

———. 2000. *HOPE VI: Community Building Makes a Difference*. Washington, DC: United States Department of Housing and Urban Development.

———. 2013. "Choice Neighborhoods Implementation Grant." https://cmhanet.com/Content/Documents/Choice_AllExhibits.pdf.

———. 2015. "Choice Neighborhoods Promising Practice Guides: Issue Brief #3: 'This is Our Community—We're All In': Civic Participation in Pittsburgh's Larimer/East Liberty Choice Neighborhood," October 2015. https://www.hud.gov/sites/documents/cnpromisingpracticeguide.pdf.

———. 2021. "Tribal Consultation for HUD Housing Counseling Agency Approval and Housing Counselor Certification Requirements, 2/4/20." HUD Exchange. https://files.hudexchange.info/resources/documents/Housing-Counseling-Tribal-Consultation-on-the-Certification-Final-Rule-Transcript-February-4-2021.pdf.

———. 2023. "HUD Proposes Expanded Support for Housing Counseling Services Tailored to the Needs of Tribal Communities," January 26, 2023. https://www.hud.gov/press/press_releases_media_advisories/HUD_No_23_016.

"Use of Donald Community Center." 2003. *New Beginnings: An Update on the Clarksdale HOPE VI Revitalization*, Clarksdale HOPE VI Revitalization, July 2003. http://www.lmha1.org/pressroom/docs/3_clarks_july_2003_newsletter.pdf.

Vale, Lawrence J. 2013. *Purging the Poorest: Public Housing and the Design Politics of Twice-Cleared Communities*. Chicago: University of Chicago Press.

———. 2019. *After the Projects: Public Housing Redevelopment and the Governance of the Poorest Americans*. New York: Oxford University Press.

"Vice President Gore Announces New Four-Part Strategy to Fight Crime and Drugs in Public Housing." 1997. The White House, Office of the Vice President, June 5 1997. https://clintonwhitehouse6.archives.gov/1997/06/1997-06-05-vp-announces-strategy-vs-crime-in-public-housing.html.

"Welcome Back 'Blue.'" 2004. *The View: The Villages at Park DuValle*, the Community Builders, Inc., Jan/Feb 2004 Vol. 3, Issue 3. http://www.lmha1.org/pressroom/docs/2_pd_jan_2004Newsletter.pdf.

West-Puckett, Stephanie, Anna Smith, Christina Cantrill, and Mia Zamora. 2018. "The Fallacies of Open: Participatory Design, Infrastructuring, and the Pursuit of Radical Possibility." *Contemporary Issues in Technology and Teacher Education* 18(2): 203–232.

"When Hope Falls Short: HOPE VI, Accountability, and the Privatization of Public Housing." 2003. *Harvard Law Review* 116(5): 1477–1498.

Wilderson III, Frank B. 2010. *Red, White & Black: Cinema and the Structure of U.S. Antagonisms*. Durham: Duke University Press.

Williams, Glyn. 2004. "Evaluating Participatory Development: Tyranny, Power and (Re)politicisation." *Third World Quarterly* 25(3): 557–578.

Wodak, Ruth. 2001. "The Discourse-Historical Approach." In *Methods of Critical Discourse Studies*, edited by Ruth Wodak and Michael Meyer, 63–95. London: SAGE Publications Ltd.

Wodak, Ruth, and Michael Meyer. 2009. "Critical Discourse Analysis: History, Agenda, Theory and Methodology." In *Methods of Critical Discourse Analysis*, edited by Ruth Wodak and Michael Meyer, 1–33. Los Angeles: SAGE.

Wolfson, Arthur M. 2005. "Lost in the Rubble: How the Destruction of Public Housing Fails to Account for the Loss of Community." *Chapman Law Review* 9(1): 51–72.

Young, Warren, and Joris Meijaard. 2002. "Political Culture, Economic Structure and Policy: The Laffont-Tirole Model Extended to Modern Japan." *The American Journal of Economics and Sociology* 61(1): 301–326.

Yu, Angus G. 2012. "Questioning the Key Techniques Underlying the Iterative and Incremental Approach to Information Systems Development." In *Project Management Techniques and Innovations in Information Technology,* edited by John Wang, 185–199. Hershey, PA: IGI Global.

Zlatos, Bill. 2012. "Mom Supported Neighborhood with Courage, Love." *Trib Live*, December 31, 2012. https://archive.triblive.com/local/pittsburgh-allegheny/mom-supported-neighborhood-with-courage-love/.

Index

About the Author

Christopher J. Morris is assistant professor of writing at York University in Toronto, Canada.

www.ingramcontent.com/pod-product-compliance
Lightning Source LLC
LaVergne TN
LVHW091531200926
848483LV00002B/369

* 9 7 8 1 6 6 6 9 4 6 8 5 7 *